When millions saw
THE SHROUD

When millions saw
THE SHROUD

LETTERS FROM TURIN

by

PETER M. RINALDI, S.D.B.

DON BOSCO PUBLICATIONS
New Rochelle, New York

Other Books by Peter Rinaldi

I Saw the Holy Shroud
Man With a Dream
By Love Compelled
It Is the Lord
The Man In the Shroud

Library of Congress Catalog Number 79-53065

ISBN 0-89944-023-1—Cloth
         0-89944-024-X—Paper

To

FORTUNE AND CATHERINE POPE

Gratefully

ACKNOWLEDGEMENTS

Like the events it describes, this book is the result of the interest and concern of many people. The author's heartfelt thanks are directed especially to the Church authorities and the International Sindonological Center of Turin, Italy. Credit for much of the scientific information goes to the *Shroud of Turin Research Project, Inc.*, for the photographs to the *Holy Shroud Guild*, the *Brooks Institute* and *Barrie M. Schwortz*, of Santa Barbara, California.

The author thanks Father Thomas McGahee, S.D.B. for designing the letterheads for this volume, including (in order of appearance) Turin's famous Mole Antonelliana, the city's tallest structure and most famous symbolic monument; the Guarini Cupola of the Chapel of the Holy Shroud; and the city's famous bronze monument to the patron of orphan boys, Saint John Bosco. The author is likewise indebted to the director and staff of *Don Bosco Publications*, for the editorial care they lavished on the book.

Peter M. Rinaldi
July 22, 1979

PREFACE

The exposition of the Holy Shroud in Turin, Italy, last fall, was a major world event which not even the momentous happenings at the Vatican, during the same period, could entirely overshadow. That nearly three and a half million pilgrims from all over the world should reverently file before the relic is itself significant. At a time when religion appears to be on the wane, particularly in such outdated forms as the cult of relics and pilgrimages, the popular response to the exposition of the Shroud astounded even the relic's most optimistic devotees.

There is, of course, more to the Turin Shroud than is generally associated with even famous Christian relics. If authentic, the Shroud is the most awesome and instructive document of Christ in existence which, indeed, deserves to take its place alongside the New Testament. For what we have in it is the most shockingly graphic rendering of the sufferings and death of Jesus that can be possibly imagined. Unbelievably, too, the Shroud reveals to us a portrait of the Saviour so unique that it has bewildered art critics and medical scientists, and has stirred millions of people.

Is it any wonder, then, that Turin should become the mecca for more visitors than it has ever welcomed since Julius Ceasar laid its foundations over two thousand years ago! For forty-three days they almost laid siege to the ancient cathedral where the relic was displayed. Among the pilgrims were hundreds of men and women for whom the Shroud has been for decades an object of study and research. It hardly seemed possible to them that the Turin church was making them welcome. For too long, they had been frustrated by the thinly disguised attitude of suspicion and hostility of its officials in their regard. Now things were changed. A congress of experts was actually encouraged and blessed by the Church authorities. Unbelievably, the Shroud itself was literally placed in the hands of qualified scientists for direct examination and tests.

This book is not meant, of course, to be anything like a history of the Shroud's exposition. It is simply a collection of experiences to which I was exposed during the two unforgettable months I spent in the citadel of the Shroud: the people, both the simple and the great who came, and saw, and prayed, and wondered . . . The little behind-the-scene intrigues that have a way of plaguing even religious events . . . The struggles to bring the Shroud out into the open in a world that believes only if it sees.

The letters were originally written to a friend. I dare not presume, but would fondly hope they will gain me some friends among the readers.

CONTENTS

I

LETTERS FROM TURIN

TURIN, JULY 24, 1978

Dear John:

This letter is long overdue. I have so many things to tell you and must do so now, before the pressure of work becomes overwhelming, as we get closer to the opening day of the exposition of the Shroud.

Let me first tell you about Turin where we are having an unusually mild summer, with none of the smog which occasionally plagues the city at this time of the year. Strolling in the park near the Po River early this morning, it felt more like spring than midsummer. A cool breeze had swept the sky clear, and the Alps, Turin's crowning glory, were a vision of majesty and beauty.

I like Turin best at sunrise when its tree-lined boulevards are free of traffic, and the light falls softly on its stately ocher-tinted buildings. It is still a beautiful city, "a city with dignity and grace," as the great English historian Edward

Gibbon described it nearly two hundred years ago. Unfortunately, both its dignity and grace are being eroded by a relentless traffic (Turin is where Fiat is based), while the new buildings, to which an exploding population gave rise in recent years, are almost an insult to the historic image of Piedmont's ancient capital.

Be that as it may, Turin as you know is the city of my childhood, and I am afraid I love it now as much as I did fifty years ago when I left it to come to America. It is quite possible that the Holy Shroud has a part in this love relationship since it is really what has brought me here. You know, of course, how deeply involved I am in the events that will soon focus the eyes of the world on Turin. But let me tell you about the latest developments.

Two weeks ago I visited Italy's former King, Umberto II of Savoy, at Cascais in Portugal. It was by far the most memorable of several meetings I had with him during the past twenty years. The Shroud, as you know, has been the reason behind these visits. Umberto owns the relic which, since 1452, has been his family's most treasured heirloom. He is genuinely interested in the scientific research which in recent years has centered on it. I well remember his words when in 1968 I asked him if I could reassure the Church authorities as to his mind in this regard.

"Certainly," he replied. "I am in favor of anything the responsible authorities will undertake with regard to the Shroud. All I ask is that I be kept informed."

The King was full of questions on the details of the exposition, anxious, too, to know what the American scientists proposed to do. I presented him with their confidential report on a detailed program of tests, and explained to him that convincing the Turin Church authorities about the need for these tests was the main purpose of my visit there.

"I wish you well, Father," he replied with a smile. "You have quite a job on your hands."

The conversation turned to other aspects of the exposition. He wondered if Turin would be ready for the event, and added in a nostalgic mood: "How well I remember the crowds at the 1931 and 1933 expositions! But people travel a lot more these days. They will probably be in

5

the millions."

"Unfortunately, Your Majesty will not be there this time," I ventured to say.

He simply smiled, somewhat sadly, I thought. He then rose, extending his hand.

"Thank you for coming," he said. "You must promise me you will return after the exposition to tell me all about it. Be sure you do!"

My visits to Umberto always leave me a little sad. They should not, really. Villa Italia where he lives on the outskirts of enchanting Cascais, is a dream of a place. He himself is always so very warm and cordial, still a handsome, vibrant man in spite of his age. But exile is a sad word, one he is never allowed to forget.

I came to Turin by way of London, and, at the risk of shamefully prolonging this letter, I must tell you what little I was able to accomplish there.

You may not know it, but helping finance research on the Shroud has been one of my less pleasant tasks as vice-president of America's Holy Shroud Guild. We had our moments of success. A substantial grant from De Rance, Inc., a Milwaukee based foundation, made possible

6

the production of *Silent Witness*, a documentary on the Shroud that has been hailed as the finest of its kind on the subject. Unfortunately, we underestimated the budget by nearly two hundred thousand dollars, a sum which had to be recouped out of the film's early revenues. It was not just the very costly program of the scientific tests on the Shroud that clamored for money. We had promised the Turin Church authorities we would assist them with the expenses of the exposition. And here we were barely a month from the event, and not a cent available.

It took superhuman efforts and some highly circuitous deals, but I left London somewhat pleased. The thirty-five thousand dollars I carried with me would be heavenly manna to Turin, not a great amount really, but a token, at least, that we were not about to forget our promise.

Incidentally, it may surprise you to know that the cathedral, where the Shroud will be displayed, is probably the poorest church in Turin. Judging from its rather imposing complex of buildings, one might not be led to believe this. But the truth is that the city's historic center, in which the cathedral is located, has been drained of its former inhabitants who were soon replaced by immigrants from the poor South, struggling to find themselves in their new surroundings.

"How can I expect these people to contribute to the Church? I have to be the one to help them." It is what their dedicated pastor, saintly Father Oreste Favoro, told me a few days ago over a cup of espresso at the humble quarters he calls his rectory.

Do not infer, my friend, that money is any real concern in the great venture of the Shroud's exposition. Surprisingly, it is no concern at all. The thrust which Turin's dynamic and beloved Archbishop, Anastasio Ballestrero, has given to the event is essentially a spiritual thrust. This is why we are all convinced the exposition will be a great success, a source of blessings, too, for Turin and for the world.

Forget the rhetoric, John, and let me take leave. I will say it the cheerful Turin way: Ciao!

Father Peter

TURIN, AUGUST 14, 1978

Dear John:

You must wonder why I have so delayed writing to you. Just plain busy, my friend! You should know, for instance, that I am still the only one around the offices of the exposition who can handle English, as well as a little French, and, of course, my native Italian. This does put some extra burden on me. Just think of the correspondence, the telephone calls, the visitors!

I need hardly tell you that the sudden death of Pope Paul VI has cast a pall of sadness on the now approaching exposition. Shortly before he died, he had written an open letter to the Archbishop praising the event. It is a remarkable document in which he not only expressed his personal interest in the occurrence, but went to great lengths to point out its meaning and importance. Let me just quote some of the more salient points of his letter.

After congratulating the Turin Church for calling the world's attention on its treasured relic, the pope adds: "We are with you in spirit, as you prepare to commemorate the fourth centennial of the Shroud's transfer to Turin from Chambery, Savoy's ancient capital, by displaying the relic for public veneration. Leaving to the scholars and the scientists full freedom for further research and study, Christians can find in the Shroud an invitation to concentrate on the Lord's sufferings and on the mystery of His redemptive mission. As we look at the distressing and yet fascinating image on the Shroud, we cannot but make our own the words of Holy Scripture: "Let us confidently approach the source of grace to receive mercy and favor and to find help in the time of need."

I am sure the point the pope made about leaving full freedom to the scholars and the scientists to research the Shroud did not escape you. He had stressed the need for this time and time again, even to the point of remarking to a Vatican friend of mine, "I can't understand why those good people in Turin are moving so slowly on the question of new exams and tests on the

Shroud. What are they afraid of?"

This much I will say: the late pope's great personal interest in the Shroud, as much as the growing popular demand and the pressure of scientists did play a part in preventing the traditionally jealous and reluctant custodians of the Shroud from postponing its exposition and examination of the Shroud any longer.

Here is an interesting footnote to the pope's letter. When told by a close associate that people in Turin were sure he would visit the Shroud, Paul replied: "I would love nothing more, but we had better leave it all to the Lord."

You must be anxious to know what is happening here now that August 26, opening day of the exposition, is getting closer. The Shroud fever is catching! Turin is putting its best foot forward, hoping the exposition will bring in at least a million people. Famed Via Roma, Turin's Fifth Avenue, never looked more beautiful, its marble columns and porticoes scrubbed and washed and waxed to a gleaming shine. Even the lovely piazzas have a new look, their monuments (every piazza is sure to have one) spruced up and bedecked with flowers. By night, the city glows.

The old Royal Palace and the stately buildings on Cathedral Square, and, of course, the cathedral itself with its domes and campanile, are spotlighted in golden light. It may surprise you to know that Turin's Communist administration has enthusiastically endorsed the exposition. In all that regards traffic, security, order, eating and sleeping accommodations for the less endowed pilgrims, they could hardly be expected to do more. I might add that they have literally opened up Turin to all kinds of cultural events, doing it, as they put it, "our way," that is, with free admission to all.

The Church authorities have done no less, of course. The Committee for the Exposition, headed by dynamic, if not always predictable Monsignor Josè Cottino, has spared no efforts and the results are for all to see. The cathedral has been literally transformed. Large steel ramps, built in the side aisles of this lovely romanesque church, will make it possible for the pilgrims to come within five to six yards of the Shroud, displayed horizontally in a bullet-proof steel and glass case into which nitrogen is fed to keep the cloth at a constantly even level of temperature

12

and humidity. Nearly all the windows in the church have been curtained. Great spotlights play on the Shroud which, totally unencumbered, will appear to the viewers as a vision of light suspended in mid air.

One of the most truly interesting things the committee came up with is the "know the Shroud" exhibit. Tastefully set up under the vaulted porticoes which surround the patio of the old seminary near the cathedral, a series of large photographic illustrations enlighten the visitor on the historical and scientific aspects of the Shroud. A visitor may know next to nothing about the relic, but by the time he leaves the exhibit, he is thoroughly informed on all its complexities.

You would be impressed at the order and good taste with which things are done in and around the cathedral. Nearly one thousand young men and women in their late teens have volunteered ·their services to escort visitors, provide information and generally assist with the movement of the crowds. I met several of these clean-cut, well-mannered boys and girls, and saw a few of them in action at the cathedral last Sunday. They are just wonderful.

Security in the cathedral is in the hands of special uniformed guards some of whom are already at work. They are efficient, courteous, but very firm. I was given a proof of this yesterday. Hawkers are not allowed in the cathedral area. In fact, not as much as a hint of commercialism is noticeable anywhere near it. When a peddler, pushing a handcart, showed up in front of the church hoping to interest visitors in a variety of holy pictures, rosaries and medals, one of the guards was soon at his side. The man began to remonstrate, but the guard, with an aplomb that might have done credit to a diplomat, escorted the peddler to the far end of the piazza. Obviously impressed with the guard's unusual manner, the ambulant merchant shook hands with him and was off to sell his wares in a more propitious place.

I hope you won't mind all these marginal details. If nothing else, they help frame the events which are central to our story. I am sure my next letter from the Shroud citadel will plunge right into it.

I shall be looking for a letter from you. Till then, Addio!

Father Peter

TURIN, AUGUST 28, 1978

Dear John:

Thank you for your letter of August 23.
I can readily see how great is your interest in all
that is taking place in Turin these days. I only
wish you were here to share in the joyous excitement.

Excitement we had, and plenty of it, last
Saturday, opening day of the exposition. At noon,
three hours before the doors of the cathedral
were open to the public, some three hundred
reporters, many of them accompanied by cameramen lugging all sorts of photographic and movie
equipment, were admitted for a first glimpse at
the Shroud at what proved to be, mercifully,
a relatively brief press conference. All of them
had descended upon Turin from Rome where
they were keeping a rather nervous watch over
the conclave. Pressed for time, they literally
stampeded toward the chancel in a mad rush to

get close to the Shroud.

It was some time before a semblance of order was restored. The Archbishop, who through the bedlam had stood unruffled in front of the microphone, was finally able to speak.

"It is only right," he said, "that you, ladies and gentlemen, should be the first ones admitted to see the Shroud. It is through you that people all over the world are being informed on what we are doing here. I should like to stress the point that the exposition of the Shroud is essentially a religious event. Though itself not directly the object of our faith, this relic is meant by its very nature to bring us to a clearer and deeper realization of the mystery of Christ, of His sufferings, death and resurrection. Were we to see it in a different light, there would be no purpose to the exposition."

He was brief and to the point, but his words were probably lost on his listeners who were soon scampering all over the place in an effort to take photographs and to interview the experts. Being, as I suppose, one of these, I, too, was subjected to a barrage of questions mostly from the English-speaking reporters. It is incredible how little

16

informed some of them were on the basics of the Shroud. Nearly all of them wanted to know if and when direct tests on the Shroud would be held, the issue of the relic's authenticity being uppermost in their minds. Luckily this point, too, had been touched on, somewhat cryptically, I must say, in the mimeographed statement I had prepared, copies of which were quickly snatched from my hands. I meekly gave into two requests for brief interviews before some television cameras, one of which was from the British Broadcasting Company, and was grateful when one of the guards approached me quietly and whispered: "Time to leave, Father. Will you please tell these gentlemen?"

I would spare you the details of the solemn liturgy with which the exposition was officially opened at 5:00 o'clock that same afternoon. What impressed me, as I mingled with the crowd that filled every nook and corner of the cathedral (the square, too, was one mass of people), was a prevailing sense of reverence. It exploded in the most moving congregational praying and singing I ever heard in my life. Archbishop Ballestrero gave a masterly homily.

"We need hardly be reminded," he said in part, "that the Shroud, however precious and venerable, is not itself the object of our faith and worship. But in order to be strong and endure, our faith needs signs. The Shroud is a sign. The disfigured image of the man we see on it tells us that the Lord Jesus, after a most painful and cruel agony, died that we might live . . . It will be well to remember, too, that we will honor Him best if we try to recognize Him in all who suffer."

He concluded by asking all present to pray for the Cardinals assembled at the conclave. He said: "How can we not possibly entrust to Him the Church He so loves?"

Leaving the cathedral, it was what people thought, what they said I wanted to know.

"What is your impression?" I asked a young woman.

"Vous parlez Français?" she replied.

"Oui, certainement!"

"I am from Paris," she continued. "I am an agnostic, or maybe I think I was. During the Mass, as I looked at the Shroud, I felt I must make a decision. With Him it's either 'yes' or 'no.' I think it's going to be 'yes.' "

From an elderly woman, a more direct, fervent reply: "It's the third time I see it. I saw it in 1931 and again in 1933. It's like meeting the Lord himself each time I see it."

A priest was equally emphatic, if a bit rhetorical. "The Shroud is a document, a photograph actually. And what a photograph! It should be in the album of everyone's life."

And a young soldier: "I am not ready to believe what people say it is, but I am glad I came."

Back in the hotel, we had stopped in the lobby and were exchanging impressions and views.

"The pope has been elected!" someone shouted.

We made a dash for the lounge just in time to see on the television screen a smiling new pope with a strange new name; John Paul I was waving his arms from a balcony, blessing the city and the world.

Indeed a day to remember!

John, I am afraid in this letter I have given you more imagery than substance. I know you are anxious to know what the Shroud experts (they are called "sindonologists") are up to these days, and what, if any new tests are planned for the Shroud before it will be put to rest once again. All I'll say now is that there are exciting things brewing, and some problems with them. I won't keep you waiting for them too long. It's a promise.

Until then, my very best!

Father Peter

TURIN, SEPTEMBER 4, 1978

Dear John:

It is quite possible the letter I am expecting
from you may reach me any day now, but here is
mine, anyway, since I am anxious to keep up my
writing schedule, and know, too, that you are
almost as pleased to read my letters as I am to
write them.

Leaving aside what you call "the spectaculars"
of the exposition (incidentally, close to a million
people have filed to date before the Shroud, and
we have more than a month to go), I mean to
keep my promise and tell you about some interesting, if at times frustrating developments
connected with the issue of the Shroud's authenticity, and, too, the problems that beset those of
us who have been pushing to open new avenues of
research.

Actually, the problems stem from the silence
with which the Turin Church authorities surround

21

the issue of new, direct scientific tests on the Shroud. One might be tempted to call it a conspiracy of silence except for the fact that there is an official explanation for it. Let me explain it to you. From the very onset, when the exposition of the Shroud was being planned, it was wisely decided to keep the religious and scientific aspects of this event completely separate. The exposition, the members of the committee declared, is to be a religious event, Christ-centered, freed of all scientific preoccupations which might only engender confusion in people's minds. The Shroud is first and foremost a Christian relic, sacred through the centuries, a "sign," a "silent witness" to Christ's sufferings and death. Let it remain so in the minds and hearts of the faithful during the period of the exposition.

The understanding was that in due time, possibly following the exposition, the scientists would be allowed their day in court. To be true, there were attempts on the part of some of the committee members to block the scientific tests altogether. For them, any and all scientists and sindonologists interested in the Shroud are meddlers out to debunk and desecrate the Shroud.

22

Fortunately, their voices were readily quashed by the Archbishop who is quoted as saying: "I will not have it said that the Turin Church closes its doors to the scientists."

No one can possibly fault the responsible authorities for wanting to keep the exposition within a religious context. What they did not take into account is that ours is a skeptic world, and that even for a great many believers the question of the Shroud's sacredness and venerability is directly connected with its authenticity. Possibly, an early official statement from the Church authorities explaining that scientific tests would eventually be held, could have clarified the issue. Instead, all mention of such tests was ruled out. As a result, dealing with news agencies and reporters became a nightmare. Something had to be done.

A week before the opening of the exposition, I telephoned Monsignor Cottino, the president of the exposition committee.

"Why don't you come and have lunch with me tomorrow," he said. "We will talk about the problem."

He was, I must say, a very gracious host, and

a good listener, too. I thought I had been fairly convincing, and finally concluded with a simple, direct question.

"Monsignor, what do you tell people who have a right to know, when they ask us if anything will be done scientifically to establish the authenticity of the Shroud?"

His answer was equally direct. "That for the present nothing has been decided by the competent authorities."

"Monsignor, does this mean that nothing is likely to be done?"

"Well now, you know that in principle the Archbishop has given the green light for these tests. They were submitted to him by the International Center of Sindonology, and that includes the tests suggested by your American scientists. But we are not ready to discuss the details, certainly not with the press. The less said, the better."

"Monsignor, as I understand these tests will be made, if at all, right after the exposition. October 8 will be here sooner than we know it!"

"My dear Father Rinaldi, you must not be impatient. You know we are not against making the Shroud available to the scientists. But first, let's get done with the exposition."

As the efficient president of the exposition, Monsignor Cottino is an extremely busy man. He is usually a kind man, though to his own admission, he can at times be very difficult. Gracious he was with me on this occasion, but I will not say that his "you must not be impatient!" was not frustrating. I am impatient, and not just because I am constantly badgered by reporters who want to know. There is more at stake. Twenty-seven scientists in the United States are committed to a program of tests on the Shroud for which they have been preparing for several months and for which they have assembled an imposing and expensive array of delicate instruments. They are making ready to come to Turin, and in Turin nothing moves, at least not in this direction.

John, say a prayer so I can be patient, since I foresee a great many more frustrations on my path before the end of this venture. Not that I do not have compensations. What I see in Turin during these days is a dream fulfilled, a dream of more than forty years, realized, too, beyond my fondest expectations. I was thinking about this tonight again after an unbelievably busy day, when, during the solemn liturgy at the cathedral, standing just a few yards away from the Shroud, I joined with some three thousand people as they sang the exposition theme song, my favorite song, incidentally, "Show us Thy Face, O Lord!"

On this somewhat emotional note, let me part with a fond "arrivederci!"

Father Peter

TURIN, SEPTEMBER 10, 1978

Dear John:

Your letter of September 3 is a joy! But, please, don't ever say again that my writing to you must add to the burden of my work. Not so, my friend. If anything, it gives me a sense of relief, a chance to sit back for a while and survey the scene around me in a sort of detached mood. It can be quite relaxing.

These are exciting days. All I know as I greet each day before dawn is that it will be a busy one, with some happy experience in store. Take the day before yesterday, for instance. I was in the midst of a busy morning at the Exposition press office when Federico, the alert and likeable factotum of Monsignor Cottino, handed me the telephone receiver. "For you, Father. From Switzerland."

"I am Tom Loughlin, Father. You might have come across my name since I am involved

27

in motion pictures and television. We know of you and were told you are in Turin. My wife and I are coming to see the Shroud with our two youngsters. We will be there late tonight, at the Hotel Principe, but must be back in Zurich by tomorrow afternoon. Can you do something so we can see the Shroud? We hear the lines are endless . . . " There was hope and urgency in the man's well modulated voice.

"No problem, certainly not for Tom Loughlin and his family. But you will have to be up early, five, no later, or you will never be able to get close to the Shroud. Here is what I suggest . . . "

It was, I knew, the very best way to see the Shroud, one that never fails to leave people pleased and grateful. It meant being in front of the cathedral at five-thirty in the morning, and join with the hundreds of hardy and devout souls who come to take part in the morning prayer service known as "Lauds," one of the Church's most impressive services.

The Loughlins, a most delightful foursome, were waiting in the hotel lobby when Paul (my nephew and truly indispensable driver) and I arrived at the Principe. We drove to the cathedral

28

through a still quiet city, barely touched by the light of a perfectly beautiful sunrise.

"We read your book on the Shroud," Mrs. Loughlin informed me. "You cannot imagine what it all meant to us. And here we are in Turin, with you!"

At the cathedral we joined the fifty or so people who were already standing in front of the locked door. They were mostly nuns, softly praying the rosary.

"It will be at least a half hour before we are allowed in," I told the Loughlins. "Let's stick together. As soon as the door opens, the five of us will form a chain holding one another's hands, with me in the lead. Be sure you follow me into the church, and don't be afraid to step lively. I will bring you right up close to the altar, within a few feet from the Shroud."

The large square in front of the cathedral was soon alive with hundreds of people who, coming from the nearby streets (no vehicles of any kind are allowed in the area of the cathedral), and walking at a fast pace toward the church, hoped to make it inside for the service. When the central door finally opened, several guards stemmed the pressure of the crowd by standing resolutely in front of it. We were among the first ones inside, and, hands linked amid the rushing people, made it quickly to the chancel where my good friend Father Mario, the cathedral's capable and beloved master of ceremonies, made us welcome to the comfortable seats around the altar. Their eyes glued to the Shroud, the Loughlins seemed not to notice anything else.

"Mom," whispered one of the girls, "I can see the picture of Jesus on the cloth. Do you see it?"

Within less than fifteen minutes, the church was one mass of people. Punctually at seven, the service began, an impressive service in which prayer and song (in flawless Gregorian chant, the choir alternating with the congregation) combined with Scripture readings. The ceremonial was monastic in its simplicity, all of it pervaded with an almost mystical touch.

As we were leaving the church, Mrs. Loughlin remarked: "Beautiful beyond words, Father! How can we ever thank you! Nearly one whole hour right close to the Shroud! And all the marvelous praying and singing! . . . "

The younger of the two girls said to me: "My Dad was crying, Father. I never saw him cry in church before."

Incidentally, this service and the solemn Mass in the evening at nine o'clock are the only two services held daily in the cathedral during the exposition. The morning service opens and the evening Mass closes the endless stream of pilgrims who, after queuing up for long hours, finally come in front of the Shroud. By groups of about a hundred or so people, they are allowed a minute and a half, during which they are given a concise description of the relic and invited to pause for a silent prayer. As many as one hundred thousand have filed before the Shroud in the course of one day. It is no wonder that the morning service and the evening Mass are attended by overflowing crowds. These are the people anxious to see the Shroud not only, but willing to "watch and pray with the Lord for one hour."

The massive queue of people to the cathedral begins to form just as the morning service ends. By then, pilgrims by the hundreds may be seen inching their way toward the barriers set up by the police, corridors actually, through which visitors are channelled toward the door of the church. A rather familiar sight are groups of pilgrims with someone in the lead carrying on a pole a sign with the name of their town or parish church. Occasionally, groups show up dressed in colorful costumes, carrying banners and singing hymns.

From noon to six o'clock every Wednesday, the cathedral is closed to the general public in order to admit the sick and the handicapped. They come by special arrangement and are carefully unloaded from a fleet of buses in front of the church. I have yet to see anything more moving than the sight of hundreds of people (as many as three thousand have been admitted in one afternoon), many on wheelchairs and stretchers, assisted by an army of young volunteers, moving slowly up the ramp toward the altar where by groups they are permitted to tarry in quiet prayer and meditation before the Shroud. I seldom miss the opportunity of being with them. It may seem odd, but few of them as much as think of praying for a miracle.

"The miracle I pray for," an old gentleman on a wheelchair told me the other day, "is that

I have the patience and strength to carry on."

The young nun on a stretcher smiled when I told her I would pray with her for her recovery.

"I look at the Shroud," she replied, "and all I think of is that He suffered, too. And how He suffered! . . . And I say to Him, 'We are in this together, Jesus. Just don't leave me.' "

"What do you think?" I asked a priest friend of mine, as we stood by the door watching them slowly come out from the dark cathedral into the bright September sunshine.

"What do I think?" he replied. "I look at those faces, so calm and serene; I hear them talk and say how happy it made them just to be here, and I say: 'That's the miracle!' "

A long letter, John. It should give you an idea of what the exposition of the Shroud is all about. The skeptics and the prophets of doom, who said that people would ignore the Shroud since these are no longer the times for such things, are stunned. Even we did not anticipate such an outpouring of faith, and are impressed as much by the tremendous crowds (amazing the number of young people) as by the spirit of faith that brings people to face all sorts of sacrifices in order to come to meet "the Lord of the Shroud."

Is there an explanation for it?

I leave you with a prosaic "I wish you were here," and a hearty "Ciao!"

Father Peter

TURIN, SEPTEMBER 16, 1978

Dear John:

In your last letter you seem to imply that life is not being very kind to me in the city of the Shroud, as if hardships were my daily lot, and frustrations my constant companions. Not at all! Turin is a very hospitable city, blessed this year with the most marvelous weather, and right now filled with people who, being Shroud pilgrims, are not only devout, but, for the most part, positively delightful.

It is quite possible my September 4 letter could have given you the wrong impression. I did mention "frustrations," but they are occupational hazards one is bound to meet in dealing with all kinds of people about problems one cannot always control. I will say, though, that it is people who are mostly responsible for the happy experiences I have been having during the first weeks of the exposition.

My nephew Paul who, providentially, is my faithful driver and constant companion, never stops being amazed. Being a rather perceptive young man, he appreciates the extraordinary variety of characters we meet, "an experience," he remarked to me the other day, "the like of which I could hardly expect in a lifetime."

So many and interesting are the encounters, it would take volumes to do justice to them. Let me tell you first about Tim and James.

I saw them early one morning as I was leaving the cathedral after Mass, just two days before the opening of the exposition. I could hear them speak English, two clean-cut boys in their late teens, sitting on the church's steps next to the sidedoor. A look at their knapsacks and sleeping bags and I knew they were pilgrims.

"Where are you from, boys?"

"Nottingham, Father."

"Hitchhikers, I take it."

"The only way, Father."

"Don't tell me this is where you slept last night! . . . "

"We did."

"And no one bothered you?"

"A policeman asked to see our passports, and all he said was, 'Buona Notte!' "

It was time we introduced one another. Timothy and James were soon free of their initial shyness.

"I know what brought you here, boys. But how did you come to know about the Shroud?"

"Ian Wilson's book," Tim replied. "It's a best seller in England."

"I know Wilson," I added. "He is a very good friend of mine. He will be here tomorrow."

"We will surely be happy to meet him," James said.

On these premises, becoming friends was easy, and just as easy for Paul and for me to take them under our wing. The steps of the cathedral were exchanged for more comfortable accommodations, while meeting Mr. Wilson and sharing in the joyous excitement of the opening day of the exposition, all helped to make their visit to Turin, in James' words, "the treat of a lifetime."

I must say I was quite impressed with the earnestness and maturity of these two fine young men.

"What is it about the Shroud that so affects

37

you?" I asked Tim over a cappuccino.

"Not easy to say, Father. Possibly, it's that it makes the Lord very real and very close, like meeting someone dear to you."

"Tim, when we first met, I had the distinct feeling that you and James might be students for the ministry."

"I have thought about that, Father," he replied with a winsome smile. "But, then, as you know, the Church does need good laymen, too. Maybe I should aim to be just that."

James and Tim left Turin two days after the exposition opened, but never quite left the hearts of many of us.

A week or so after the opening of the exposition, I went back to the press office late one morning after a busy two hours at the cathedral, dealing mostly with a reporter from Time magazine.

"A cardinal has been looking for you. He is now at the Maria Ausiliatrice church," the secretary told me matter-of-factly.

"And who is the cardinal?"

"I really would not know. So many cardinals have been coming to Turin . . . "

When I arrived at Maria Ausiliatrice, the young man who greeted me at the office said:

"You must be Father Rinaldi. Two cardinals have been looking for you."

Meeting my good friend, Cardinal Cooke of New York and my old classmate, Cardinal Silva from Santiago, Chile, compounded my joy. Later, I accompanied them on a courtesy visit to the Archbishop of Turin. It was a very cordial meeting, most of the conversation bearing on the Shroud and on the new pope.

"His Excellency the Archbishop might consider letting us have the Shroud after the exposition. It would be wonderful if we could expose it at St. Patrick's Cathedral in New York." Cardinal Cooke seemed quite serious about the request. When I translated his words into Italian for the benefit of Archbishop Ballestrero, his eyes and hands raised in a gesture of doubt and surprise, "Oh," he said, "this the Turin people will never allow. They would be afraid the Shroud will never come back. They know! They never did give it back to Chambery after they got it here under some pretext four hundred years ago. No, I am afraid we won't let go of it."

The visit with the two Cardinals was not the only reason for which I welcomed the opportunity to see Archbishop Ballestrero. After the two prelates left, I stayed on for the talk I was anxious to have with him.

"Your Excellency," I said, "as you know, things are going extremely well with the exposition. We are also making excellent progress preparing the Congress of Sindonologists. But frankly, I am concerned with regard to the examination and the tests you authorized on the Shroud."

"What seems to be the trouble, Father?"

"Nothing moves, not here in Turin, anyway. The American scientists are committed to do their very best. A great deal of preparation, money, too, has gone into this project. I get phone calls nearly every day from the States. They are anxious to know if Turin is ready for this operation."

"Are the people at the International Center of Sindonology, and is Monsignor Cottino aware of this? Have you been in touch with them?"

"I have, Your Excellency. I am not making any headway with them at all. You might put in a good word . . . "

"I will, of course. I thought I had made it clear from the start that the scientists were to have a free hand with regard to the tests that have been authorized. I don't think you need worry, Father."

If you remember, John, you too told me not to worry in one of your recent letters. It does feel good when nice people like you and the Archbishop say it!

My very best regards!

Father Peter

TURIN, SEPTEMBER 24, 1978

Dear John:

Thank you for your letter of September 15. You say the nicest things about my letters, but you should know by now that it gives me great pleasure to keep you informed on events that mean so much to us both.

I can see you are as anxious as ever to know what, if anything, will be done to advance scientific research on the Shroud. By now you must surely have my letter of September 16 in which I quoted Archbishop Ballestrero's words on his firm decision to "allow a free hand to the scientists." There is more good news.

The other night, in the sacristy of the cathedral, just a few minutes before we walked to the altar for the solemn liturgy, Monsignor Cottino assured me we were finally on the move. The last hurdle had been removed when the detailed list of the instruments to be used for the tests

42

was approved by the scientific commission of the International Center of Sindonology. They had previously screened the forty or so scientists (twenty-seven are Americans) who will work on the Shroud.

"As soon as the scientists arrive from the States," Monsignor Cottino explained, "we must arrange for a meeting. The work has to be coordinated with our scientists here." He then added with one of his rare smiles, "You do look pleased, if I may say so, Father Rinaldi."

I was. In fact, I don't think I remember singing and praying with greater elan than I did at the Mass that night.

Though not yet publicized, here are the tests presented for approval to the Archbishop by the scientific commission of the International Center. I might add that these tests, now approved, are the very ones our American scientists suggested to the Center.

1. Electronic microscopy with neutronic scansion to determine the presence of blood or other substance on the Shroud.

2. Radiographic examination; X-ray fluorescent examination; microphotography; infra-red

photography; ultraviolet photographs: spectroscopy; complete coverage with photographs in black and white, and in color.

3. Removal with magnetic tape of surface particles from the Shroud in order to isolate more pollen grains, and also to obtain other material for exact and definite testing.

4. Removal of several threads from various parts of the Shroud, particularly the stained areas, for scanning electric spectroscopy and ion microprobe examination.

5. Extensive examination of the reverse of the Shroud.

An official press release on these tests will be given on October 6, two days before the closing of the exposition. The tests should begin at midnight, October 8, and continue through several days.

And now back to some more "spectaculars." By police count, we are well passed the two million mark in terms of visitors. It is easy to note that they are increasing as we move toward the end of the exposition. At six o'clock this morning they were already lined up for nearly half a mile. You might also like to know that some thirty cardinals and nearly three hundred bishops have venerated the Shroud to date. Pope John Paul I has signified his deep regret that he will not be able to come due to pressure of work in these early days since his election. As archbishop of Venice, he had planned to lead the pilgrimage from his archdiocese. And he did in a way. When the Venetians, nearly two thousand strong came to Turin a few days ago, he was indeed in the lead. A young man, in full Venetian medieval regalia, proudly led the procession of pilgrims holding high on a pole a large portrait of smiling John Paul.

Speaking of bishops, all of twenty of them showed up together, and all of them Americans. They came to Turin via Rome where they had visited with the new pope. When I notified Monsignor Cottino (as president of the exposition committee, he is also the official receptionist) they were due, he thought I was joking. "Twenty bishops all at one time!" he exclaimed. "Don't you bring them to my rectory for dinner!"

We met in the sacristy of the cathedral before they were escorted to see the relic. What I especially liked about these unassuming, cordial men is that they appeared to be anxious to know about the Shroud as they were to see and venerate it. Even bishops cannot be expected to be proficient on all the complexities of this relic, and so they were full of questions as each of them scanned the sheet with the Shroud's photograph I had given them. Incidentally, this excellent map of the Shroud, properly diagrammed with legends in five languages, is placed in the hands of every pilgrim as he or she steps into the cathedral. This makes it possible for them to identify the images as well as other stains and markings which can be somewhat vague and intriguing to the person who sees them on the Shroud for the first time.

The bishops were admitted to the steps of the altar over which the Shroud is displayed. They were thus even closer to the relic than the people who looked at it from the ramp. I was much impressed by their devotion, sincere and unaffected. All of them knelt for several minutes, some of them quite evidently moved. Their comments outside were revealing. Said one of them: "I felt as if I had before me not an image, but a presence, like at Mass after the consecration." Another, speaking to a fellow bishop, "John," he remarked, "did you notice the expression on the faces of the people who were standing on the ramp looking at the Shroud? Absolutely ecstatic!"

I do not know how ecstatic this lengthy letter will leave you, but, as with all my letters to you, I am glad I wrote it.

As the Italians say it, "saluti affettuosi!"

Father Peter

TURIN, SEPTEMBER 29, 1978

Dear John:

It is late, nearly midnight, after a long day
that began with the shocking news of the sudden
death of Pope John Paul I. Writing to you may be
good therapy, for I am still numb, unable to
absorb mentally and emotionally that the "smiling Pope" is dead.

Even the Shroud has receded into the back-
ground. When this morning, at the prayer service
in the cathedral, the pastor, Father Favaro,
informed the overflowing congregation that the
Pope had died suddenly during the night, a gasp
and cries of "no! no!" ran through the church.
People just left off singing, and a stunned silence
fell over the crowd, broken by muffled sobs.

Tonight's liturgy was offered for Pope Luciani.
"We do not have the wisdom to know what lies
behind this saddest of events. Of one thing we
must be convinced: the Lord knows what is best

for His Church. Let us not be dismayed, but renew our trust in Him." It was the way Archbishop Ballestrero put it in his moving homily, which tells it all, but does not remove the ache from the heart.

By now you must have my September 24 letter with all the good news about the scientists on the Shroud. The scientists due from the States will arrive tomorrow, all twenty-seven of them, several with members of their families. These days have been busier than ever for me, since the logistics of arranging their two-week stay in Turin have fallen to me. Thank God for Paul who is much more than a nephew and a driver to me. I would be lost without him.

With all I must attend to and contend with, I have not been able so far to rid myself of one perrennial source of annoyance: reporters. If anything, they seem to grow and multiply by the day, and manage to pursue their quarry everywhere.

"I am a pest," one of them told me recently. "Please, be nice to me."

One such cornered me in the hotel lobby last night.

"I heard the American scientists are due in Saturday," he told me. "Surely you can tell me something about the tests on the Shroud."

"There will be an official press release next week," I replied. "No, there is nothing I could possibly tell you."

"Please, Father, I promised my paper I would have a story this weekend. Couldn't you at least answer one or two questions?"

"Not about the tests."

"Can we sit down for a moment?"

"But not more than one or two questions, and not about scientists or tests."

"This may sound a bit rash. What if the tests were to prove that the Shroud does not date back to Christ?"

"Science would even have a greater mystery on its hands. It still would have to explain the image on the cloth, a negative image, with no visible trace of either paint or dye; and an image which, when photographed, turns into the most incredible portrait of Christ ever seen."

"But what will happen to the faith of millions if the Shroud is found not to be authentic?"

"Nothing whatever. Christian faith rests on

God's word, not on the Shroud. It is not the Shroud that makes me believe in Jesus; it is rather my faith and love for Him that makes me revere the Shroud. The Church never officially proclaimed nor will she ever proclaim the authenticity of the Turin relic. She leaves it to science to decide."

"But the Church does honor and revere the Shroud . . . "

"Like she does any and all sacred images. But note, too, that the images, however sacred (and that includes the Shroud), are not themselves directly the object of our faith and worship. We venerate the persons they represent. In the case of the Shroud, it is Christ."

"But why does the Church move so slowly in allowing scientists to examine and test the Shroud?"

"The Church always moves slowly. But move it will, this time."

"Can I quote you on this?"

"You may, of course!"

There may be low points even in an exciting adventure, and being badgered by reporters may well be one of these low points. However, in no way does this cancel the happy experiences the exposition of the Shroud constantly provides. The story behind one such experience is so unique I just must make room for it in this letter.

It all began in a small village in Gloucestershire, in England where in 1955, Josie Woollam, an eleven-year old child dying of a severe bone disease, suddenly knew she would be cured, "if I could just touch the Shroud." Unbelievably, she was permitted to do so, the pope and former King Umberto of Savoy having taken a direct interest in the matter.

On July 7, 1955, Josie was in Turin. Removed from its vault over the altar, the silver chest which contains the Shroud, is unlocked, something done only two or three times in the course of a century under the most extraordinary circumstances. Josie reaches out from her wheelchair and places her hands on the cloth. Strangely, she is suddenly drained of all desire to be cured." All I wanted," she said later, "is for people all over the world to come close to the Shroud so they can come close to the Lord."

Two weeks ago, she was back in Turin, accompanied by the man she calls "my guardian angel," retired RAF officer Leonard Cheshire, a war hero who has since devoted his life to rebuild shattered lives all over the world. It was Captain Cheshire who in 1955 introduced Josie to the Shroud and to a new lease on life. A tiny whisp of a woman, Josie, now Mrs. Jones, could hardly speak when interviewed by reporters.

"It's the Lord I came to thank in Turin," she said. "The miracle I asked for as a little girl turned out to be many miracles. I am well, as you see. I have a wonderful husband and a dream of a child. Even this visit to Turin is a miracle, since I could never have come but for the kindness and generosity of Captain Cheshire."

I sat along side them during the Mass that evening in the cathedral, only a few feet away from the Shroud. They were in tears most of the time.

"Can heaven be more beautiful, Father?" she asked me.

At that point I was not thinking of heaven. I was looking at the mass of humanity assembled in the church, and of the hundreds of thousands of people who, during these days, come to this church to look, to think, and to pray. I was thinking, too, of the words a little girl said after she touched the Shroud twenty-three years ago. "All I want is for people to come close to it so they can come close to Jesus."

It is, you will agree, another experience to treasure for the rest of my life. Having shared it with you, I find it easier to part and to say, "fare thee well, my friend!"

Father Peter

TURIN, OCTOBER 4, 1978

Dear John:

I am back to burning the midnight oil again, or I will never be able to squeeze this letter through the maze of work this last week of the Shroud exposition is weaving for me. When my nephew came to pick me up at six o'clock this morning, I said to him: "Paul, only eighteen things to do today!"

"Not bad," he replied with a smile. "Didn't we have nineteen yesterday?"

It is always the first appointment I like best of all, the morning service at the cathedral which I attend daily, usually in the company of special pilgrims who need a little extra assistance to get in. Would you believe it? This morning I had five semi-cloistered nuns in tow.

"You haven't missed one service yet," jovial, smiling Father Mario, the cathedral's master of ceremonies, said as he welcomed me and my guests in the chancel, near the altar.

"Why should I, Father Mario? This service makes my day."

Let me brief you on the latest events. Our American scientists arrived Saturday. Fortunately, we are all in the same hotel, not more than an eight-minute walk from the cathedral. It is not a place of great luxury, but it's clean, comfortable and quite pleasant. I know all those fine men, and many of their wives, too, since we met at various seminars in the States. A splendid group, they are extremely well prepared for the job. Just think, they went through a dry-run of the entire operation before they left the United States. They are eager to start, and have met several times to plan on all details since they have arrived.

We were about to begin one such meeting last night in one of the hotel conference rooms, when Monsignor Cottino walked in. With him were Monsignor Caramello, a palatine chaplain representing King Umberto, and Professor Luigi Gonella, of the Turin Polytechnic Institute, who is the coordinator between the American team and the European scientists. After exchanging very cordial greetings, Monsignor Cottino moved that the conference take up its work.

Professor Gonella speaks English fluently, a great asset in an operation of this sort. It did not take him long to realize how well prepared the Americans were. Our men were likewise impressed with the Professor's grasp of things. The careful report on each test, detailed in a fine brochure, and the slide presentation of the dry-run of the entire operation were evidence enough that the tests, so long and minutely prepared, had all the guarantees of success.

I knew this was the moment of truth, and my eyes were constantly on Monsignor Cottino. He appeared impressed and pleased. I remember he had frowned somewhat when I once mentioned to him the special rotating frame or table the scientists had designed and built for the Shroud.

"I just hope," he had told me, "they are not going to mishandle the relic by pinning it on all sorts of support."

"No pinning at all," I replied. "Just magnetic tape, and only that one frame for the entire operation."

Seen on the slides of the dry-run, the frame, with a mock-up of the Shroud stretched on it, easily convinced the good Monsignor that it was indeed the very best thing for the relic. Once secured to the frame, the relic required no more displacing since it could be moved to any position by simply rotating the frame.

We finally came to the most crucial point. How much time would the scientists be granted for the tests? Here, too, I recalled the first reaction from some of the Church officials when I broached the subject to them.

"We just can't envisage the Shroud under all those lights for hours on end. We would expect twelve hours should be more than enough, twenty-four, at the very most."

I remember remarking meekly that the Shroud would be exposed for forty-three days, constantly under far more powerful lights.

They had an answer to that. "The protecting crystal of the frame was especially made to filter the light."

The tests, as programmed, required at least one hundred hours. Professor Gonella proved to be as convincing as he was competent. I held my breath when Monsignor Cottino finally asked to speak.

"Gentlemen," he said, "let me just tell you what the Archbishop told me on this point. 'All the time the scientists need, but not one minute more.' "

A warm applause greeted his words.

Among other details discussed was the place in which the tests were to be held. It had already been decided it would be one of the inner rooms of the Royal Palace which adjoins the cathedral.

"You gentlemen," Monsignor Caramello said, "are welcome to take a look at it tomorrow. You must keep in mind that the Royal Palace is a seventeenth century building. The room is probably more artistic than functional."

Monsignor Cottino stood up. "Just two more things before we leave," he said. "They are of the utmost importance. This operation may well be compared to what goes on in a hospital operating room. You know, of course, that none but the surgeons and the needed attendants are admitted. What I mean is that no one will be as much as allowed inside the palace who has no business being there. Special passes are being prepared. The guards will be inexorable, and so will I and the palatine chaplains in charge. High-placed people and very worthy clergymen, some of my best friends in fact, have been refused admission. This is as much a matter of policy as of security. And here the second thing: there is to be no publicity whatever, no communication to the press. I hear they have started to hound you already. Just tell them an official statement will be made next Friday. Thank you, gentlemen, and good-night."

One more hurdle stood suddenly and ominously before us: persuading the Italian Customs agents in Turin that we needed those seventy crates of instruments (they had arrived from the States two days before) immediately, not in two or three weeks. Finally, Professor Gonella decided to be less diplomatic. To the punctilious official who perversely kept insisting that several days would be needed to release the shipment, he said:

"Do you realize what is likely to happen if we should have to cancel those tests because of your delaying tactics? An international scandal! The press will really go to work on it, and Italy's impossible bureaucracy will become the laughing stock in the world."

This may or may not have helped, but the

fact is that the wheels started to move. In little more than two hours, a terse message came over the phone: "Your shipment has been released."

We were finally really on the move! You must have done your share of praying, John. Keep it up. The adventure is far from over.

As always, my very best to you.

Father Peter

TURIN, OCTOBER 9, 1978

Dear John:

I can finally write to you in a relaxed mood, the kind I have not known since the beginning of August. The exposition is over, and so is the Sindonological Congress which was meant to be an appendix to the exposition, but turned out to be a tour de force that had us extremely busy right up to the end.

What is not over are the tests on the Shroud. They are being held right now in the sanctum of the Royal Palace, and have been going on around the clock since midnight Sunday. But more about them later.

It is the congress I'd like to tell you about. Like the tests, it was intentionally kept in the shadows for fear it might conflict with the essentially religious character of the exposition. For this reason, too, it was held on the last two days of the exposition, October 7 and 8.

The credit for the success of this seminar belongs to Turin's *Centro Internazionale di Sindonologia*. I might even go further and state unequivocally that the Center was, through years of quiet work, the driving force behind the exposition itself.

It may surprise you to know that the members of the Center are nearly all laymen with a splendid tradition of devotedness to the Shroud. A permanent museum of Shroud memorabilia and other priceless Shroud documents was expanded during the exposition, and was visited by thousands of pilgrims. A prestigious multilingual review, named Sindon, is published by the Center, and serves admirably to link together the many national Shroud groups throughout the world, affiliated to the Turin Center.

The Reverend Piero Coero-Borga is the general secretary, the very soul of the Center. Working closely with Count Angelo Lovera di Maria, the president, and assisted by the Center's members, Father Coero-Borga organized and steered the congress, the second international seminar on the Shroud, since 1950.

The congress was held in one of Turin's

finest congress halls, equipped with a perfect instant translation system in several languages. Attended by nearly four hundred sindonologists, it was chaired by Professor Giorgio Cavallo, the distinguished president of the University of Turin. Over a two-day period, twenty-five papers were presented, followed by lively discussions.

What did the congress aim to accomplish? Briefly, its purpose was to place before the religious and scientific world the results of the most recent studies on the Shroud. Practically every discipline connected with the relic came into play as well-known sindonologists took their place at the lectern. Spare me the details. As one interested in the Shroud, you should by all means secure the volume of the congress proceedings soon to be published.

The new tests on the Shroud were not themselves a direct concern of the congress, but on them centered the interest and a good deal of the conversation of the congress participants. The statement to the press which the Archbishops's office released on these tests was read to the assembly and warmly applauded. Some eyebrows were raised, and even some voices at the part of the press release which referred to the Carbon-14 dating test. It stated: "The Carbon-14 test has not been requested and will not at this time be included among the tests."

It was felt by some that this position was totally unwarranted. Father Coero-Borga, of the International Center which had submitted the various tests to the Archbishop for approval, stood his ground. He said:

"The decision not to include at this time the Carbon-14 test was not arbitrary. We simply do not have at this point a consensus from the experts on the unqualified validity and efficacy of this test in the specific case of the Shroud. A prerequisite is that only minimal parts of the cloth be used. The moment we will have this assurance, and not just from one source, we will certainly move on this test."

The "one source" referred to by Father Coero-Borga is the University of Rochester, N.Y., whose laboratory is headed by Professor H. E. Gove, who was present at the congress. Addressing the participants, Professor Gove agreed that Father Coero-Borga was right in

65

wanting a consensus of experts before a Carbon-14 test is made on the Shroud. And he added:

"Obviously, like other experts on the Carbon-14 test, I am in no hurry to test the Turin Shroud. But we want it known that we are available for such a test, using minimal parts of the cloth, just a few threads actually."

"Will samples from the Shroud be available?" Someone asked Father Coero-Borga.

"We have some already," he replied, "and more will be extracted from the Shroud before it is returned to its vault."

So the issue on the Carbon-14 dating test is still hanging, and we should hear a great deal more about it in the near future.

Time to put an end to this letter, John, but not before I tell you about one more experience.

While we were preparing for the congress, a letter reached us at the center office that had us amused and somewhat perplexed. We were actually berated by the angry writer who wrote:

"What do you sindonologists hope to accomplish? If the Shroud is authentic, then it is a gift of God, and you people should stop meddling with it. If it is a forgery of some sort, then you are wasting your time."

I thought I owed the irate correspondent the courtesy of a reply, and here, as best as I remember, is what I wrote to him.

"Sindonologists, sir, are a persistent lot. They will simply not let go of the Shroud. Some of them are quite convinced that the mystery of the Shroud will never be solved, but this in no way lessens their fascination for it. If anything, it becomes an even greater challenge to them."

I then proceeded to tell him where I stood on the issue, adding:

"I personally like to see science "meddle" with the Shroud, but I hope—in fact I am quite sure—science will never be able to solve its mystery of Jesus. Like the Man of Nazareth, the Man of the Shroud will continue to disturb men's minds and trouble their hearts. And that," I concluded, "is the way it should be."

And, John, this concludes this long epistle, too.

Till next time, addio!

Father Peter

TURIN, OCTOBER 13, 1978

Dear John:

Surely you must have noticed the fast pace of my letters lately. It is the only way I can make them keep up with the events now rushing headlong toward the end.

I have just returned from a visit to the "NASA Room" at the Royal Palace. You may wonder, but such indeed is the name a leading Turin daily has been using when referring to the room in which, since midnight Sunday, the Shroud is being subjected to the most thorough examination present day technology can provide.

Monsignor Cottino, watchdog supreme of the entire operation, has relented somewhat, and a few privileged ones are being quietly admitted to the palace' sanctum.

"You really did not think I would keep you out, did you?" he said with a smile when we met, shortly after ten o'clock tonight, on the first landing of the palace's great marble stairway. We were soon walking through a long ornate corridor toward what he called the "operating room."

"I am positively amazed at the way these men are performing," he remarked. "They are serious, precise, and efficient. They certainly know what they are doing. It's crushing work, too, around the clock. Fortunately they work in relays."

Power cables were snaking everywhere on the beautiful parquet floors. Then suddenly, the room. And the Shroud.

It looked absurdly out of place in those surroundings. The great Holy Relic, which for six weeks had been displayed like a vision of light in the cathedral, the focus of millions of eyes and hearts, was now stretched on a stark steel and aluminum revolving frame, looking fragile and vulnerable, surrounded by a battery of strange machines, a half dozen men working feverishly over it. Looking at the faint image on the cloth, I almost felt as if I were in the presence of a sick, helpless friend.

The men nodded to me, but went right on

with their work. I was watching fascinated when one of them invited me to peer through what appeared to be binoculars, but were actually part of a large camera, moving horizontally on a track, some two inches from the Shroud. He explained to me that the camera literally photographed every inch of the cloth.

"Look through the viewers, Father, and note the extent of the magnification."

The threads of the fabric actually appeared as lengths of cord, criss-crossing one another, with tiny empty spaces between them.

"You are looking at a section of the Shroud which is not where the image is," he told me. "Let me now move and focus the camera on a portion of the Shroud where the image is."

The threads still appeared as lengths of cord, though somewhat darker, the spaces between them still empty, not a trace of pigment or any other substance in them.

By midnight Friday, when the work will be completed, some thirty thousand photographs and slides will have been made of the Shroud. The word "photograph" is somewhat restrictive, since there is a great deal more involved in these tests. Spectroscopy, X-ray fluorescence, infra-red photography, X-ray radiography, microphotography, all had a part in the operation. Said one of the scientists:

"We are interested, among other things, in the distribution of the color spots that form the image on the Shroud fibers, and how they can be related to the chemical processes, if any, that took place at the time the image was formed. We are extremely well equipped to do this."

But they have been using other procedures, too. For instance, working with an especially prepared adhesive tape which was applied to the cloth, it was possible to lift from the Shroud surface samples the nature of which can be identified through microanalytic tests. This, too, can lead the scientists to unlock the secret of how the mysterious image was produced on the cloth.

The American scientists are working closely with the Italian group, Professor Gonella and Professor Pier Luigi Baima-Bollone of the Institute of Forensic Medicine at the Turin University, acting as coordinators between the two groups. Swiss Professor Max Frei, too, has been part of the team. You may remember his amazing discovery of pollen grains on the Shroud during the 1973 examination of the relic. This internationally known criminologist is now seeking to expand his experiments to confirm the evidence that the Shroud, at some time in its history, was indeed in Palestine, Asia Minor, Turkey, and, of course, France and Italy.

It may come as a surprise to you, as it does to many, to hear that the reverse of the Shroud has not been examined or even seen for over four hundred and seventy years. Following the fire at Chambery in 1532 which substantially damaged the cloth, the nuns of St. Clare, concerned to strengthen the Shroud where it was burnt through and through, decided not only to sew patches on the twelve fairly large damaged portions of the relic, but first backed the entire Shroud with another linen sheet, and then sewed the patches on to this backing cloth as well to provide greater firmness. They then carefully sewed the new cloth all around the edges of the Shroud. Unstitching the backing cloth from the Shroud becomes an extremely hazardous task which no one up to now has attempted to do, fearing the Shroud might literally come apart.

What has been done now is unstitch a fairly large portion at one corner of the Shroud which does not include any of the patches. A fiber fluoroscope was introduced between the Shroud and the backing cloth, thus making it possible to inspect the back of the relic. A specially built fluoroscope camera likewise made it possible to photograph practically the entire reverse side of the Shroud.

What is in back of the Shroud? The nuns who patched it four hundred and fifty years ago wrote that the same image which could be seen on the front of the Shroud is also visible on the back, "only much fainter," which leads experts to believe that whatever impression is on the back may be just the front image seen by transparency. This seems to have been confirmed by the fact that the threads extracted from stained portions of the Shroud show coloration only on the thinnest surface of the fiber, its inner part not being stained in the least. The optical fluoroscope examination made last Monday was not decisive. It is possible that the photographs will solve the mystery.

It will take time, possibly as long as two

years, to make an evaluation of all these tests. With this in mind, I was being more than premature, rash actually, when I hazarded a question to one of the men who has been researching the Shroud for years and who had a part in most of the tests made so far.

"Not a fair question, to be sure," I told him, "but neither do I expect anything like an unqualified reply from you. Tell me, from what you men have seen during these past three days, would you say that we have just a little more light on the mystery of the Shroud?"

His answer was prompt and unequivocal. "I would say, Father, that, if anything, the mystery becomes even greater."

One more searching, reverent look at the Shroud, a parting word to Monsignor Cottino and to the men, and I left the palace after one more unforgettable experience.

Time to sign off, John, less this letter, too, like some of my former ones, grow to indecorous proportions.

Ciao, amico!

Father Peter

TURIN, OCTOBER 17, 1978

Dear John:

I have your letter of October 9, in which, among other things, you tell me that the news coverage of the Shroud events has been somewhat less than expected. This may be due, in part, to the fact that the spotlight in recent weeks has been constantly on the momentous Vatican events. There were certainly enough reporters and television cameramen in Turin when, on Sunday, October 8, the exposition closed. The excitement was even greater than on opening day.

Now all is quiet here, with almost a touch of sadness in the air. Everybody has left, or so it seems. The American scientists and their families were the first ones to go. What delightful people! The Archbishop, who met several of them at the Royal Palace during the tests, told me later: "Splendid men indeed! Efficient, capable, and yet so very friendly and unassuming!"

In a way, the Shroud, too, has left us. In the dead of night between Friday and Saturday, October 14, the cloth, carefully rolled up like a scroll around a circular wooden mast, was placed in its silver chest. Carried to the cathedral's Royal Chapel, it was securely locked (three separate keys are used) in its vault over the altar. The thirty or so people who were present all offered a silent prayer, I am sure, that the relic will not be kept buried in that vault for another fifty years.

"Why," asks a reader of the Turin *La Stampa*, "why deny people the spiritual joy and comfort millions came to seek during the exposition? The Shroud should be exposed at least once a year at Easter time, or some other appropriate time. Modern technology can easily provide for its safety and preservation. Better still, if it can be arranged to have it permanently displayed. Who can deny that the exposition gave Turin a spiritual lift? It brought us all closer to the Lord and to one another. Let it continue to do so!"

To this I say "amen" with all my heart.

I am afraid this letter will be somewhat disjointed. There are so many things that remain to be said about this magnificent adventure that I will probably end up by scattering them in every direction. I never told you, for instance, that the exposition did face some opposition from rather unlikely sources. Surprising but true.

These opponents were not all anti-church people. Loudest among them were some Catholic groups, even clergymen who saw in the exposition of the Shroud a form of outdated obscurantism and fanaticism. They claimed the Turin Church was distracting Christians from what is central to their faith, Christ's message of salvation and His stress on love and concern for one's neighbor. The cult of relics, they said, belongs to a past in the Church which Vatican Council II sought rightfully to erase from people's minds.

I will say that this hostile position misjudged completely the intent behind the exposition which was truly Christ-centered, and totally devoid of any form of pietism, let alone fanaticism.

"No one as much as asked to light a votive candle," the pastor of the cathedral told me.

"Anyway, we had none available."

As for any outburst of fanaticism, there was not a semblance of it at any time during the exposition. Reverent, orderly, if anything too quiet, hundreds of thousands of people filed before the Shroud without betraying any particularly strong emotion other than occasionally moving their lips in prayer or blessing themselves. In some rare instance, eyes filled with tears during the short few moments people spent in front of the relic. Whatever they felt became an inner experience most of them, if questioned, would express in such words as, "I felt as if I had been in His presence," or "I thought of Him suffering for me," or "I just felt deeply moved." A young man in jeans said: "I never felt anything except terribly sinful."

The Christ-centered character of the Shroud exposition came through in the positively marvelous liturgies held in the cathedral during the exposition. The words in the Mass, "This is my body which will be offered for you; this is my blood which will be shed for you," took on new meaning and force when pronounced or heard with the Shroud before one's eyes.

78

All this may sound a bit preachy, John, but I am sure you are one to appreciate the rationale behind such an event as the exposition. Let me just make one more point. The opponents of what they called "a sterile cult of relics" were convinced that Christians whose faith, as they put it, reaches out to fetishes and feeds on them are not likely to value Christ's message of love and concern for others. All I need say is that not one sermon was preached at the cathedral during the exposition that did not touch on love and concern for one's neighbor. Incidentally, people were constantly reminded that the collection offerings were destined for the developing countries. Even the theme song of the exposition was keyed to this idea. Here is the song's refrain:

> Your Face, O Lord, I seek.
> I see in it the faces of all who suffer,
> And I hear you say,
> "Comfort them and you comfort me.

I must tell you an amusing story about this very point.

We were in the sacristy of the cathedral late one night, after the solemn Mass, helping the nuns whose task was to attend to all details connected with the liturgy. It was no mean task, incidentally, since no less than two hundred priests concelebrated at the Mass every night. The former Archbishop of Turin, Cardinal Pellegrino, had presided at the service. In his sermon he had stressed once again the importance of recognizing in the image of the Shroud not only the suffering Lord, but those who most resemble Him, our suffering brothers and sisters.

"The Man on the Shroud," the Cardinal said, is the man you probably ran into on the way here tonight, whose anguish was written all over his face, but for whom you did not have a glance to spare." We were discussing these words while working in the sacristy when someone suggested:

"Aren't we carrying this a bit too far, I mean this constant repeating that the face of the Man on the Shroud is the face of every man?" Surprisingly it was a little nun speaking. She continued:

"The children are getting a bit confused. They are beginning to ask if the image on the Shroud is Jesus or every man. We don't know what to tell them anymore!"

"Maybe we should tell them it's both," the pastor suggested quietly.

Well, John, it is as good and true a story as any with which to bring this letter to a close. I think you agree that the Shroud does touch people's lives in all sorts of ways. I might get back to this in my next letter and maybe try to explore the mystery behind it. If I read you correctly, you more than hinted in one of your letters that you would want me to do so.

Till then, my warmest regards!

Father Peter

TURIN, OCTOBER 23, 1978

Dear John:

This will probably be my last letter to you from Turin, at least for a while, since I expect to be leaving tomorrow for a bit of rest on the hills of Monferrato, at the foot of the Alps, where, they tell me, the last of the vintage is yielding the tastiest grapes ever picked in that famous wine region.

I am anxious to get back to you on a point you brought up in one of your recent letters. You wrote, if you recall, that you were amazed that the Shroud should arouse so much interest in the world, and wondered what lay behind it. I would say that the obvious reason is that the Shroud interests the scientists almost as much as it does the average religious person. One of America's leading sindonologists, Doctor John P. Jackson, of the U.S. Airforce Academy, Colorado Springs, writes: "That the Shroud, a religious relic, should become a challenge to the scientist is itself extraordinary. And just as extraordinary is the fact that it should involve practically every branch of science known to man."

"I stand in awe before the Shroud," wrote Yves Delage, a member of the French Adademy and a self-styled agnostic.

And Doctor Pierre Barbet, a highly esteemed surgeon at the Paris Institute Catholique, confessed: "At first I was amazed, then bewildered, and now I am fascinated."

From the photographer who stands astonished before the incredible negative image he sees on the Shroud, to the art expert who is unable to explain the unique portrait of Christ which derives from that negative; from the pathologist who, in the realism of the wounds and bloodstains of the Man of the Shroud can identify him easily with the Crucified One, to the NASA scientist who is faced by a totally unexpected three-dimensional portrait; from the Scripture scholar who reads on the Shroud a perfect version of the Gospel narratives of Christ's passion, to the historian who seeks to trace the Turin relic back to Calvary; all who have ever approached the Shroud with an open mind agree that it exerts on them an irresistible fascination. "I simply cannot detach myself from it," again to quote Doctor Jackson.

Some people are convinced this fascination is induced by the power, the serene majesty and virile beauty of the face of the Man of the Shroud, as photography reveals it. Paul Claudel, philosopher, poet and art critic, says of this face: "It is not just a portrait. It is a presence." I have had people say to me: "I don't need scientists to tell me the Shroud is authentic. All I need is to look at that face."

All of which is undeniably true. Yet, precisely because of my experience or experiences during the exposition, I am convinced that something more is at work here. It is, briefly stated, the fascinating mystery of Christ Himself. In this context, I would place His own very words: "When I will be lifted up on the cross, I will draw all men to me."

You might tell me that here we are treading on dangerous mystical ground, but, in my long life as a priest, I have yet to discover that mysticism and reality are necessarily contradictory.

And so, John, to answer your question, "What draws people to the Shroud?" I will simply refer you to those words again, "On the cross I will draw all men to me."

I am also convinced He still keeps drawing them to Himself in all kinds of ways, through the Shroud, too. I did not go looking for proofs of this during the exposition. I found them at every step, even if not all of them made for as moving an experience as I had just a few days before the exposition closed.

It had been one of my busiest days at the cathedral. One more group of visitors from Canada, then the Mass, and I would finally be able to call it a day. I was standing in the middle aisle of the church where people could tarry in prayer while the great mass of pilgrims, channelled through the ramps in the side aisles, were inching their way to the chancel to see the Shroud at close range. I was somewhat struck by the sight of a young woman who, seated in one of the pews with a pad on her knees, appeared absorbed in thought, occasionally bending to write. I asked one of the volunteer workers if she might not possibly be a reporter.

85

"All I know," he replied, "is that she has been here the last two or three days. She comes in around four in the afternoon, and then stays right on for the Mass. She only speaks English."

With this, I decided to approach her. "Nice to meet someone who speaks English," I said.

She appeared delighted. "I have seen you before, Father, and heard you speak English, but never picked up quite enough courage to speak to you."

"You really do not need courage to do that."

She smiled. "I am from London, and will be leaving to go back tonight. I am a free-lance writer, but not really looking for a story."

"Something must have brought you to Turin . . ."

"What else?" she pointed to the Shroud. "I guess He came looking for me and found me. It was through a book on the Shroud, too. You must think I am some kind of a fanatic. Not so, Father. I even wonder I should have reacted the way I did when I read that book, and saw that face, since I was as far from Him as anyone could be. My life, in fact, was in shambles, religiously, morally and every other way. Now it is all changed. It's as if I had just begun to live. When I heard about the exposition, I knew I had to come. I felt I owed it to Him.''

There were tears in her eyes.

"I can't tell you," I said a bit clumsily, "how happy I feel just to have you tell me these things.''

"Thank you, Father. Will you remember me in your prayers if only to thank Him for me?''

Before I even had a chance to speak again, the young volunteer was at my side.

"Excuse me, Father," he said, "your group is here. They are waiting for you.''

A smile, a parting gesture, and another experience in my life.

Late that evening, in the cathedral, now silent and dark but for the light that shone on the Shroud, I stopped as usual by the altar to take leave of the security guards and to offer a quiet prayer. I did not think it at all odd that the day's moving experience should suddenly come to my mind. And, too, the words of a young woman whose life had been "in shambles," had told me: "I guess He came looking for me and found me.''

The melodrama is not my doing, John. It is built right in the story, the way it comes through. Anyway, I hope I have replied to your question, even if it took a lot of words to come to the point. What it really all adds up to are the words already quoted: "I will draw all men to me."

This being my last letter, parting becomes just a little harder. I know you believe me when I tell you that writing to you has been a joy, and that my "Arrivederci" this time is the most cordial ever.

Father Peter

II

THE

SHROUD

IN

PICTURES

Fig. 1. Clovio, a sixteenth-century artist, depicted this scene of the Saviour's burial, showing how His body's image came to be imprinted—front and back, head to head—on the linen in which it was wrapped. Clovio was familiar with the relic which he had seen in Turin.

That Jesus was given a hurried, temporary burial is clearly implied by the Gospel narratives. "The Sabbath was imminent" (Luke 23:54), and so was the period of the hallowed rest. The bereaved disciples limited the burial operations to a minimum. The fact that after the burial, "the women returned home to prepare spices and ointments" (Luke 23:56) implies that the body had not been anointed. Still unprepared for the definite burial, it was laid upon one half of the "clean Shroud" and covered with the other half drawn over the face. The Shroud, purchased by Joseph of Arimathea on the spur of the moment (Mark 15:56), had been profusely spread with spices provided by Nicodemus (John 19:29), evidently intended to slow down the process of decay. Joseph thus "wrapped the body in the clean linen Shroud and put it in his own new tomb" (Matt. 27:60)—there, adds John, "since it was the Jewish Day of Preparation and the tomb was near at hand" (John 19:22).

As scientists examine the incredible imprints on the Turin Shroud, they ask: How did they come about? What did happen in the silent darkness of the sepulchre? . . . Research is currently more intense than ever on the enduring mystery of the Shroud.

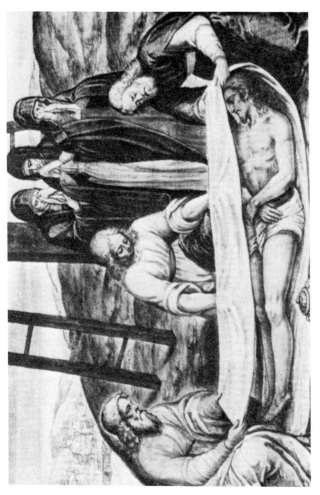

Fig. 1. "Joseph who bought a Shroud, took Jesus down from the cross, wrapped him in the Shroud and laid him in a tomb hewn out of rock" (Mark 16:46).

Fig. 2. For the last four hundred years, the Holy Shroud has been the most treasured relic of this 14th century romanesque church. It is enshrined under a towering dome of black marble in the Royal Chapel behind the chancel of the cathedral from which the chapel interior can be seen through a wall of glass panels.

The chapel, whose architectural style has no equal in Europe, was built especially for the Shroud by the Savoy family, owners of the relic since 1452. Access to the magnificent shrine is provided by two great marble staircases on either side of the cathedral chancel. The chapel is also directly connected with the royal palace, residence of the members of the House of Savoy, Italy's royal family until 1946.

The recorded history of the Shroud dates back to 1353 when Geoffrey de Charny, a warrior in the 12th Crusade, built a church at Lirey, in the north of France, in which he placed "the true burial cloth of the Lord." Prior to its Lirey sojourn, the whereabouts of the Shroud are often only a matter of conjecture. In 1452, Geoffrey's granddaughter, Margaret de Charny, presented the relic to the Dukes of Savoy who kept it on their Chambery estate until 1578 when they transferred it to Turin, newly chosen capital of their states.

Fig. 2. The Cathedral of Saint John the Baptist in
Turin, Italy.

Fig. 3. After centuries of vicissitudes, the Holy Shroud came to rest on this monumental altar, beneath lofty arches of black Spanish marble, surrounded by baroque statuary and ornaments. Princes of Savoy have their tombs here, among them Emmanuel Philbert who in 1578 ordered the Shroud to Turin from Chambery, Savoy.

Carefully rolled like a scroll around a velvet-covered spindle, the Shroud is kept in a long narrow silver chest, lined with cedar wood and velvet, safely stored in a vault enclosed by iron bars, high on the altar beneath the great black marble dome. Here people from all parts of the world stop to pray and to meditate on the Passion of Christ.

Public showings of the Holy Shroud have been extremely rare. It has been generally and quite properly felt that frequent handlings and exposure tend to impair the cloth. During the present century, the relic was exposed for public veneration only three times, in 1931, in 1933, and in 1978.

Fig. 3. The reliquary of the Holy Shroud in the Royal Chapel, adjoining Turin's cathedral.

Fig. 4. It was the longest exposition of the Shroud ever held in its history. From August 26 to October 8, three and a half million people came to Turin to see and venerate Christendom's most famous relic. No single event ever attracted so many visitors to Piedmont's capital. Though a stately and beautiful city, once known as the "Italian Paris," Turin is not a common tourist spot for the tens of millions who annually visit Italy. It has few points of interest to rival neighboring Milan, or other northern cities such as Venice or Florence. The visitors who came to see the Shroud were quiet, prayerful people.

They came from all over the world. "Like being in St. Peter's Square on Easter Sunday," remarked a seasoned pilgrim while waiting in line, as the endless queue, fifteen to twenty abreast, quietly, patiently and reverently inched their way toward the cathedral.

For most of them, seeing the Shroud became a deeply felt experience which they often tried to express with such words as, "Like meeting the Lord Himself . . . " Or, "The closest I ever felt to Him!"

Fig. 4. When millions saw the Shroud. As many as one hundred thousand pilgrims per day visited the Shroud during the exposition.

Fig. 5. Some three hundred reporters gathered in the cathedral on the opening day of the exposition to hear and question Turin's Archbishop Anastasio Ballestrero, and chairman of the exposition Monsignor Jose Cottino. They were eager to photograph the Shroud, too, never before photographed or videotaped by such an imposing array of reporters.

Traditionally reluctant to say much about their relic, the two Church officials expanded on the religious character and thrust of the exposition, but were politely evasive with regard to the scientific issue. It would be dealt with later, after the exposition during which, in the words of the Archbishop, the Christ-centeredness of the Shroud would be the only concern.

Said Archbishop Ballestrero: "Not itself the object of our worship, the Shroud is a sign of our faith. The disfigured image of the man we see on it speaks to us of the suffering and death of the Lord Jesus . . . It will be well to remember, too, that we will honor Him best if we try to recognize Him in all who suffer."

Fig. 5. The world wanted to know. The press conference on the opening day of the exposition.

Fig. 6. Stretched horizontally in a bulletproof case (the Shroud was kept at an even temperature and protected against moisture by an inert gas constantly fed into the glass housing), the 14'3'' long and 3'7'' wide relic, flooded by a soft golden light, appeared like a vision of light, suspended in mid-air, in the encircling semi-darkness of the cathedral. The effect was startling.

Though somewhat distracted by the singed portions of the cloth, the patches, water stains and creases, the eye was irresistibly drawn to the faint shadow-like imprints of the Man of the Shroud. The two hundred or so pilgrims, who in turn stood for little less than two minutes gazing at the relic, were instructed briefly by a guide on the meaning of the imprints, and then invited to offer a silent prayer. When gently reminded it was time to leave to make room for the next group, they kept their eyes riveted on the cloth even as they slowly moved away.

As many as one hundred thousand persons each day saw and venerated the Shroud in what has been described as the largest gathering of persons ever to take part in a religious event.

Fig. 6. What the pilgrims saw. The Holy Shroud appeared like a vision of light in the darkened cathedral.

Fig. 7. An examination of the Shroud by experts, involving direct and thorough testing of the cloth, was what Shroud devotees and scholars had prayed for since the day photography revealed the astonishing characters of the imprints on the Turin relic. The preliminaries to such testing came in 1969, when a commission of experts did indeed examine the Shroud, probing into the cloth from which minute samples were extracted and analyzed. It was a breakthrough in the Shroud's research which provided substantial new evidence in favor of the relic's authenticity.

Science's greatest hour for the Holy Shroud struck at midnight, October 8, when, following the exposition's closing ceremony, the relic was transferred from the cathedral to a large room in the nearby royal palace. Complex and delicate instruments (eight thousand pounds of them shipped from the United States) had been set up in this room. For five feverish days and nights, forty scientists, twenty-seven of them Americans, subjected the Shroud to all kinds of tests, including microphotography, spectroscopy, X-ray fluorescent analysis, optical spectrum scans, infra-red and ultra-violet photography. Magnetic tape samples of particles from the cloth were extracted as were actual threads for microanalysis. The mass of data collected would provide material for many months of study and research. Will science solve the enigma of the Shroud's astonishing image?

Fig. 7. Science and the Holy Shroud. The Shroud in the "laboratory" following the 1978 exposition.

Fig. 8. By heightening contrast, photography gives us here a far more vivid and intense image of the Man of the Shroud than is actually seen on the cloth. On the ivory-tinted linen, the image appears like a faint sepia stain which appears and vanishes like a delicate shadow or a misty vision. There are no clearly defined edges to the image or any of the other signs of human craftmanship which are always present in man-made art.

Strikingly visible are the marks left by an accidental fire at Chambery, in 1532: two dark streaks running the length of the linen, water stains, and patches sewn on portions of the burnt cloth. But the eye is easily drawn to the shadow-like double imprints of a human body in the center of the Shroud. See Fig. 1 for the manner of burial that produced the frontal and dorsal imprint of the Man in the Shroud.

These imprints are like images on a negative. They are, in fact, negative pictures, reversed in light and shade, and position. We know they are negatives because photography gave us the positive version of these images, revealing the true nature and significance of these mysterious stains, as may be clearly seen on Figure 9.

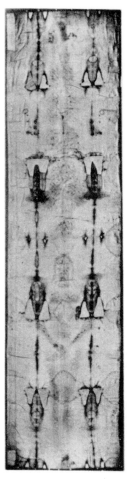

Fig. 8. A full view of the Holy Shroud as it appears to the eye.

Fig. 9. We have seen that the imprints of the body of the Man of the Shroud are shown inverted on the cloth (Fig. 8). They are negatives. Photography proves this, reinverting the negative imprints of the cloth into positive images. In so doing, photography gives us a true photographic portrait of the Man the Shroud enveloped.

The picture on this page faithfully reproduces the negative of the Shroud's photograph. Let the reader examine this picture. On it, the image of the Man of the Shroud has become positive. Let him now compare it with Fig. 8. He will note that the inversion from negative (the body imprints in Fig. 8) into positive (the body imprints in Fig. 9) is complete as to lights, shades and positions. Only the body imprints (negative on the cloth) have become positive. The linen itself, its singed portions, patches and creases have turned negative as have the bloodstains imprinted on the cloth by direct contact. They are dark on the Shroud, and consequently appear light or white on the negative.

But it is especially to the face of the Man of the Shroud that we would direct the reader's attention. Let him compare the face in Fig. 8 with the face in Fig. 9. Better still, let him compare Fig. 12 with Fig. 13. It is here that the Shroud's "negative-into-position process" stands revealed at its best. Can the Man of the Shroud be other than Christ?

Fig. 9. The Holy Shroud as it appears on the negative plate or film when photographed.

Fig. 10. Since we have on this picture the positive version of the Shroud image, the Man of the Shroud appears here as he looked when wrapped in the cloth. It has been stated that in all the history of pictorial art, there is no example that could even remotely compare with this portrait.

The anatomical perfection of the body portrayed on this picture, and the uncanny realism of its minutest details are all but incredible. Medical men who examine this photograph detect in it the perfect characteristics of a corpse, above all that of RIGOR MORTIS. They are certain that the Man of the Shroud died while hanging by the arms. The expanded rib cage and the drawn-in epigastric hollow point to that. It is also evident that he was scourged and that his head was pierced by sharp points; that he was nailed through the hands and feet, and lanced in the right side.

The marks of these wounds are easily detected: the wound on the left wrist (contrary to all pictorial tradition which invariably shows the nail wounds in the palms), the trickles of blood on the forearms and on the forehead, the splotch from the wound in the body's right side. Visible, too, are the marks left by the scourges over the entire body.

It is no wonder that a famous Paris surgeon should write: the idea that an artist, centuries ago, should have conceived, let alone painted, in the negative, such an image is too preposterous even just to think about it.

Fig. 10. The frontal image of the Man of the Shroud as it appears on the negative when the Shroud is photographed.

Fig. 11. Here, too, the anatomical proportions of the entire back of the Man of the Shroud (as it appears in its positive version) correspond perfectly with the frontal imprint. The details are just as striking. At the top, is the spot on which the head of the Man of the Shroud rested. It is profusely marked by trickles of blood from the crown of thorns which must have been shaped like a cap.

Especially noteworthy on this dorsal view of the Man of the Shroud are the scourge marks. Indeed, the scourge left traces of its gruesome work over the entire body, front and back, but it is on the dorsal region that these marks are particularly numerous. The scourge bit through the flesh and left traces of itself in the shape of tiny double knobs. The lashes (about 125) are generally distributed in twos or threes, and appear as they had been inflicted at random, chance or the caprice of the lictors deciding the direction of the blows.

In the region of the shoulder blade, medical experts detect a mass of escoriations, suggesting the weight and friction of what must have been a rough beam. They believe the condemned man was forced to carry only the horizontal beam of the cross, somewhat balanced across his shoulders. One more detail on this "positive" of the Shroud's dorsal image: the strikingly visible imprints of the legs and feet. They are turned somewhat inward, toward each other, suggesting the position of the feet on the cross. Note, too, how the left leg appears shorter and bent at the knee. This would imply that the left foot was nailed over the right one, one nail piercing both feet at once.

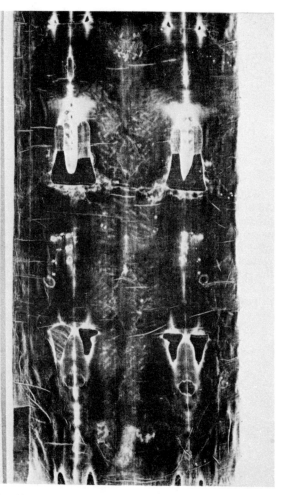

Fig. 11. The dorsal image of the Man of the Shroud
as it appears on the negative when photographed.

Fig. 12. THE FACE OF THE MAN OF THE SHROUD AS SEEN ON THE CLOTH OF TURIN—On the Shroud, the face, like the entire body, appears inverted, like a negative, with no detectable trace of paint or dye. Experts agree that no artist can possibly paint a negative portrait, perfectly reversing lights, shades, positions, and even the expression such as we find in this image. See it now on Fig. 13 as it appears on the negative, reinverted into its positive values by the photographic process.

Fig. 13. "IT IS THE LORD!" This incredible portrait of Christ appears on the negative plate or film when the inverted (negative) image on the Shroud is photographed. It is a positive picture so uniquely perfect that experts find it difficult to believe it is actually on the Shroud, reversed on the cloth, like a negative. Says art-expert, Dr. C.D. Viale: "That so incomparable a portrait of Christ should be found IN REVERSE on an ancient linen is an enigma to which we art-experts have no solution."

Fig. 12. THE FACE OF THE MAN ON THE SHROUD

Fig. 13. "IT IS THE LORD!"

Fig. 14. That the image on the Shroud is three dimensional was first discovered by American scientists through a computer process. Speculating that the image must in some way reflect the three-dimensional surface of the body the Shroud enveloped, they decided to convert all image points to proper vertical relief, using the Interpretation System VP-8 Analyzer. The result was an amazing three-dimensional brightness surface of the image. The procedure has since been adopted by other experts who have obtained equally surprising results. The photograph shown here was processed by Prof. Giovanni Tamburelli, of Turin, Italy.

Scientists believe that the unique three-dimensional quality of the Shroud image proves beyond doubt that the Turin relic must indeed have been wrapped around a human corpse whose volume contours were encoded in the varying intensity levels of the image. If this were not so, the three-dimensional quality would not be present in the image with such astonishing perfection. Experiments show that conventional paintings and photographs, when computer-analyzed, give very disappointing results, the three-dimensional quality, when present at all, being highly distorted.

Fig. 14. The Face of the Man of the Shroud as revealed
by the computer.

Fig. 15. The nuns from the Order of St. Clare have had more than casual associations with the Turin Shroud. After the Chambery fire in 1532, members of the Order were asked to make extensive repairs to the relic substantially damaged by the fire. In 1973 nuns from the same Order were summoned to assist the experts in extracting threads from the cloth and two tiny pieces from its edges, later used for analysis.

The recent examination of the relic of necessity included the reverse of the Shroud. Strange as it may seem, the back of the cloth had not been seen by anyone since the Chambery fire in 1532. In the process of patching the burnt portions of the relic the nuns, to provide extra firmness to the cloth, backed the entire Shroud with another linen sheet. The patches which they sewed on the Shroud they also stitched onto the backing cloth. They then carefully sewed the new cloth to the edges all around the Shroud.

In the picture, the two St. Clare Sisters are shown unstitching the backing cloth from a section of the Shroud. Only a part was unstitched lest the frail linen suffer further damage.

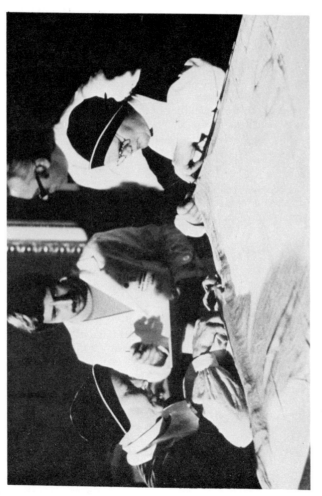

Fig. 15. Sisters of the Order of St. Clare preparing the Holy Shroud for the tests.

Fig. 16. The instruments used during the examination of the relic were the best modern technology can provide. Nearly all the scientists on the team had delved beforehand into the complexities of the Shroud through months of research and study. They are of mixed religious faiths, including Catholics, Protestants, Jews and Mormons, and some are agnostics. They represent a large number of scientific disciplines.

As one of them put it: "It is easier to arrive at truth when you have a number of overlapping disciplines involved. Science can't really lie. It is difficult to impose emotions or misinterpret scientific findings. In the agreements we signed, we have pledged ourselves not to use any of the information for any commercial purpose, nor to sensationalize it in any way. When completed (because it is privately funded it may take two years to complete the work), it will be published in a special volume."

Speaking to Father Rinaldi about these scientists, Monsignor Jose Cottino who, as chairman of the exposition, followed their work almost hourly during the examination of the relic, had this to say: "I am positively amazed at the way these men are performing. They are serious, precise, efficient. They certainly know what they are doing. It's crushing work, around the clock, but they are extremely well organized."

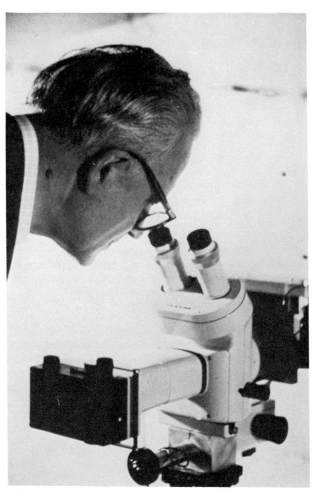

Fig. 16. The author, Father Peter M. Rinaldi, examines the Holy Shroud through the viewers of a powerful microphotographic camera.

Fig. 17. "Miracle" was not a word Church officials
welcomed during the exposition of the Shroud. No such
claim was made by any of the thousands of sick and
handicapped people who came to visit the relic in organized groups each Wednesday afternoon.

"We are not looking for the Lourdes' type of miracles," commented one of the priests at the cathedral. He
added: "If these good people draw strength and comfort
from seeing the Shroud, and it is quite evident they do,
then that is the miracle."

The case of Josie Woollam Jones, whose story is told
in these pages, is in a class by itself. Speaking of the day,
years before, when she, a dying eleven-year-old girl,
was permitted to touch the Shroud, she could say with
tears in her eyes: "It's the Lord I came to thank in Turin.
The miracle I asked for as a little girl turned out to be
many miracles. I am well, as you see. I have a wonderful
husband and a dream of a child. Even this visit to Turin is,
in a sense, a miracle, since I could never have come but
for the kindness and generosity of a very special friend."

III

ABOUT THE SHROUD:

YOUR QUESTIONS ANSWERED

WHAT PEOPLE ASK ABOUT THE SHROUD

What first revealed the Shroud to the world?

A photograph, in 1898. Secondo Pia, who was authorized to photograph the Shroud for the first time in its history, was astonished to note on his negative plate an impressive portrait, quite evidently the positive picture of the dead Christ, exact in every detail and endowed with a marvelous expression. He wondered how it could have derived from the blurred, dim imprints barely visible on the Shroud. Gradually he understood. If the picture on his negative plate was a positive (and it was, unmistakably), it could only be because he had photographed a negative.

Incredible as it may seem, it was true. This meant that Christ's portrait was on the Shroud, though it was there in reverse, exactly as on a negative. By turning the Shroud's negative into a positive picture, Pia's photograph had revealed the Saviour's body exactly as it appeared when laid in the sepulcher. Since 1898, other photographs have been made of the Shroud which revealed even better the astonishing characters of the Turin relic.

Is the Shroud mentioned in the Gospels?

The Scripture scholar approaches the enigma of the Shroud with caution. In their Gospel narratives, the Synoptics (Matt. 27, 59; Mark 15, 46; Luke 23, 53) mention a sindon, a linen cloth, bought and used for the burial of Jesus, a cloth which all interpreters claim must have been a large sheet well within the dimensions of the Turin Shroud. St. John's Gospel does not specifically mention a large cloth, but does not exclude it. John simply writes: "They wrapped Him in linen cloths with spices" (John 19, 40).

Luke is careful to note that the linens were in the empty tomb when Peter came and "could see nothing but the wrappings" (Luke 24, 12). John is more specific and minutely describes their position (John 20, 8), clearly implying that they (the shroud itself and other smaller cloths customarily used at burials) were not in disarray, as they might have been had thieves snatched the body from the tomb. It was, in fact, the sight of the linens that convinced him that Jesus had indeed risen. "He saw and believed" (John 20, 8).

What does history tell us about the Shroud?

The historian is the Shroud's worst enemy. He is less than satisfied with the documents that purport to link the Turin Shroud with Calvary, and tends to see in it a pious medieval forgery of some sort. The Turin Shroud, he claims, has no history beyond the fourteenth century. It is only since 1353, when it first appeared at Lirey, France, that reliable documents record its existence.

True, but historians do admit that Christ's burial cloth, bearing the imprint of His body, was known long before the Turin Shroud became Europe's most treasured and discussed relic. The image of the Lord on a cloth, "an image not made by hand," *achiropoeton*, was one of the great living traditions of Eastern Christianity, as the icon of Edessa and other revered icons testify.

127

Europe's earliest pilgrims to the great shrines of the East mention the burial cloth of Jesus as being first in Jerusalem and later in Constantinople, where the French Crusaders found it when they sacked the city in 1203.

Admittedly, history can only prove that the Turin Shroud could be Christ's burial cloth, not that it is. This is why the relic was destined to be an abject of dispute until science and applied technical skill came to support its claim to authenticity.

Why has the Shroud, so long ignored, become so important to Christians?

Through the centuries, the Shroud was never a major concern of the Church. With the Holy See the authenticity of the Shroud is not an issue *per se*. It is left to the scientists to decide. In its official pronouncements and prayers about the Turin relic, the Church does not as much as hint that Jesus left on the Shroud the imprint of His body. What is said is that "we venerate the image of the Lord visible on the Shroud."

It is only since science took a direct interest

in the relic that the Church has been under pressure to take action, as was demonstrated in the recent exposition. Science has literally catapulted the Shroud to the foreground in the Church. The implications are for all to see. If authentic, we have in it not only a material document of the historical existence of Christ, but a visually graphic evidence of His sufferings and death, and, at least indirectly of His resurrection. What is more, the image on the Shroud, when photographed, shows us in its dark simplicity, how Jesus appeared to men. It is a portrait which amazes artists and stirs millions of people, truly overpowering in the calm, serene majesty of death.

What do the scientists tell us about the nature of the Shroud's mysterious imprints or images?

To determine the nature of the images on the Shroud is precisely what the scientists are currently trying to do. Both the European and American researchers aim to expand the range of the discoveries made by the 1969 commission. The great many tests, made after the recent exposition of the Shroud, will undoubtedly lead to interesting results. This much is known: the microstructural analysis of samples extracted from the Shroud has not so far revealed the presence of blood on the cloth. There is no pigment whatever on the Shroud, and the tests thus far have not isolated or identified any substance that could be responsible for the image formation. Another surprising thing came up during the tests: whatever the coloring substance that stained the image on the Shroud, it covers only the thinnest surface of each thread. No penetration or absorption and no diffusion is noticeable. The Shroud image appears to be purely a surface phenomenon.

Are we to conclude, then, that neither direct contact of the body with the cloth nor any conceivable chemical action could have stained those images on the Shroud? Is it possible that they may have been produced by some process akin to photography? In other words, that a violent burst of some form of radiation, be it light or heat, could have impressed this incredible negative image on the Shroud? It is all, for the time being, interesting speculation. The answer may well be found in the thousands of photographs, photomicrographs, spectrograms, X-ray fluorescent and infra-red photographs assembled during the recent examination of the relic.

So much has been made of the three-dimensional quality of the image on the Shroud. Does it actually prove anything?

That the Shroud image is three-dimensional was discovered by American scientists through a computer process. Doctor John P. Jackson and Doctor Eric Jumper, professors of the U.S. Airforce Academy, Colorado Springs, speculating that the image on the Shroud must be equivalent to the three-dimensional surface of the body wrapped in the Shroud, decided to convert all image points to proper vertical relief, using Interpretation System's VP-8 Image Analyzer and an IBM 360/50 computer. The result was an amazing three-dimensional brightness surface of the image.

This proved beyond doubt that the Shroud must indeed have been wrapped around a human body whose volume contours were encoded in the varying intensity levels of the image. If this were not so, the three-dimensional quality would not be present in the image with such astonishing perfection. Experiments show that conventional paintings and photographs, when computer-analyzed, give very disappointing results, the three-dimensional quality, when present at all, being highly distorted.

The scientists are likewise convinced that the three-dimensionality of the Shroud image could not have been formed by direct cloth-body contact, since in such a case, the Shroud would have been stained only where the cloth touched the body. Indeed, so distinctive and unique is the three-dimensional quality of the Shroud image that no medieval artist or forger could possibly encode it in his work.

Is it true that medical scientists are the staunchest defenders of the Shroud's authenticity?

Doctors agree, first of all, on the fundamental proposition that the image on the cloth of Turin is not an artistic endeavor of any kind, but the imprints of a human corpse, one which has been crucified.

The anatomical correctness, the perfect realism in minutest details of this corpse is what astonishes medical men as they examine the entire unclad body whose frontal and dorsal imprint can be seen on the Shroud. Among the Shroud's details that not even a present-day artist with the most consummate knowledge of anatomy and physiology can produce, medical men include the following: the perfect characteristics of a corpse in the condition of *rigor mortis*, with the added evidence of one who died while hanging by the arms, such as the abnormally extended rib cage, the distended lower abdomen, the sharply drawn-in epigastric hollow, etc.

Doctors next point to the transfers of blood which are uncannily true to nature, including the separation of serum from the cellular mass. The mark of the nail wound on the wrist, rather than the palm, is against all pictorial tradition. Even the stains of blood from the head, both front and back, (evidently caused by the crown of thorns that covered the head like a cap) are so very natural that, upon seeing them, a practitioner of forensic medicine remarked to me: "These are actual photographs of blood." No less realistic are the marks left by the scourges, the nailed feet, and the large gash in the side made by the spear. Despite decades of efforts, the opponents of the Shroud have not succeeded in proving a single violation of the laws of anatomy and physiology in the image of the Shroud. Doctor Pierre Barbet, after years of intense study and research on the Shroud's image, believes the medical scientist needs no other evidence to be convinced of the authenticity of the Turin relic. He concludes:

"The idea that an artist of the fourteenth century could have conceived, let alone painted or stained these negative images is sufficient to disgust any physiologist, any surgeon. Please, don't even talk about it! This image is proof enough that nobody has touched the Shroud except the Crucified Himself."

What do art experts and critics say about the image on the Shroud?

They agree that the portrait of the Man on the Shroud cannot be an artistic production. It is, first of all, the negative character of the image that baffles the art expert, a negative so perfect that, when reversed by the photographic process, the result is all but incredible. Writes Doctor V. Viale, director of the civic museums of Turin:

"We cannot as much as suppose that this picture could have been produced by a medieval artist when, even today, with our knowledge of positive and negative, no artist can reproduce the human figure in negative, particularly a face, preserving on it so delicate a thing as the expression while reversing its lights, shades and positions."

It is interesting to note the two portrait artists of renown, Reffo and Cussetti of Turin, made replicas of the Shroud working directly from the cloth. So skillfully did they portray the imprints as seen on the Shroud that, looking at them, one might believe he is actually looking at the Shroud. However when photographed and seen on the negative, the positive version of these painted imprints was a complete disappointment. The images appear so distorted, the face especially, as to be barely recognizable.

When asked whether the Shroud image might

betray a pictoral style proper of any art period or school of art, Doctor Viale replied: "The Turin Shroud is truly in a class by itself. There is no other example in iconography, either in the East or in the West, which could even remotely compare to it. In all my years of experience with pictorial productions, I have yet to see anything that approximates the image on the Shroud. That so incomparable a portrait of Christ, with no detectable trace of paint or brushwork, should be found in reverse, as a negative, on an ancient cloth is an enigma to which we art experts do not have a solution."

Is it possible that the images on the Shroud may be due to a miracle?

A miracle is an event that appears unexplainable by the laws of nature, and is held to be supernatural in origin. Is it necessary to postulate a direct intervention of God in the case of the Shroud? Would it not be more logical to believe that there can be a natural explanation of some sort to the formation of the Shroud images, but not exclude, at the same time, the providential concurrence of the unusual circumstances that accompanied the death and resurrection of Jesus?

On this point, Geoffrey Ashe offers an interesting theory. He writes:

"The Christian Creed has always affirmed that Our Lord underwent an unparalleled transformation in the tomb. His case is exceptional, and perhaps here is the key. It is at least intelligible (and has indeed been suggested several times) that the physical change of the Body at the Resurrection may have released a brief and violent burst of radiation, perhaps scientifically identifiable, perhaps not, which scorched the cloth. In this case, the Shroud image is a quasi-photograph of Christ returning to life, produced by a kind of radiance or incandescence analogous to heat in its effects. Hints of some such property are supplied by narratives of the Transfiguration and the blinding of Saul."

Doctor David Willis, from whose study "Did He Die On The Cross?" the above has been quoted, rightly concludes:

"Perhaps in our present state of knowledge, that is as good an explanation as any. It is consistent with the present conception of matter as forms of energy, and, too, the fact of radiation images formed on stone following the dropping of the atomic bomb at Hiroshima. It also ties in with Leo Vala's conviction that the Shroud image is in some way "photographic." Vala is a brilliant inventive photographer. As an agnostic, his conviction is impressive. He writes: "I can prove conclusively that claims calling the Shroud a fake are completely untrue. Even with today's highly advanced photographic resources, nobody alive could produce the image — a negative — embodied in the Shroud."

What do the scientists hope to discover as they delve into the data gathered at the Shroud's recent (October, 1978) examination?

Briefly, the enigma of the image on the Shroud. Since the most recent tests have laid to rest the theory that this image could be an artistic production of some sort, the question remains: "How was it formed on that cloth?"

The image, which on the linen looks little more than a blurred shadow, is an incredibly perfect negative. When photographed, it registers on the negative film as the most stunningly detailed and impressive positive portrait of the Crucified ever known. What caused it? Since it is a purely surface phenomenon (no identifiable substance penetrated the cloth), it has been suggested that the image might have been seared on the fabric by a burst of radiation which accompanied the "flash of lightning," mentioned in the story of the Resurrection (Matt. 28, 3-7). Experts decline to speculate. But can we blame them for not leaving any stone unturned in their effort to discover the nature and origin of this uniquely mysterious image?

Why hasn't the Carbon-14 dating test been applied to the Shroud? Will the responsible authorities ever permit it?

Until fairly recently, a sizeable portion of the Shroud was required for this test. It is understandable that the owner and the custodians of the relic should want to move slowly on a test that involved partial mutilation of the Shroud, all the more since there were some reservations about the one hundred percent validity of this test in the specific case of the Shroud. It is known that the relic was exposed to unique vicissitudes in its long history. It was nearly baked, as well as partly burnt, when the silver chest in which it was kept was engulfed in flames at the Chambery, Savoy fire in 1532.

During the recent exposition, the responsible authorities were unable to obtain a consensus from the experts on the unqualified efficacy of the Carbon-14 test, a prerequisite for which is that only minimal parts of the cloth be used. Since the quantity of material needed for the test has considerably lessened in recent years, and, according to the experts will continue to lessen, and, too, since for a valid test several samples must be used from different parts of the Shroud, it was prudently decided to postpone the test for the time being.

"Minimal" samples (threads, actually) were extracted from the Shroud before it was returned to its vault last October 14, precisely with a view to their being used for such a test. For a test so crucial and definitive, the officials have programmed not just one, but several laboratories, and have asked them to experiment first with other linens that date with certainty to the time of Christ.

Have the experts come up with anything startling thus far?

The work of analyzing the vast amount of data, gathered from the direct examination of the Shroud, is understandably slow, particularly since the scientists must do it on a volunteer, sparetime basis, due to lack of funds. Results will not be published until all the data have been processed, which means not for several months. Preliminary results, weighed by the scientists at a recent meeting (March, 1979), proved exciting.

"Any evidence of forgery is positively out," said one of the spokesmen for the team. "Had we discovered elements pointing to a fraud, we would have walked out the door long ago."

"It would be miraculous if it were a forgery," said Professor Donald Lynn, head of science operations for the Jet Propulsion Laboratory's (NASA) Voyager's project.

Doctor Raymond Rodgers, a microchemist at Los Alamos Scientific Laboratory, was even more emphatic. "When asked to examine the cloth in Turin, I was fifty percent sure I would walk in, spend thirty minutes or so looking at it, and decide it was a hoax, not worth wasting our time on it. Not so at all. I am convinced the burden of proof is now on the skeptic."

He added: "The image is a light-scattering phenomenon. You see it best at a distance. As you get close, it is harder and harder to detect. When you put a microscope on it, you can hardly find it. There is no earthly way we can explain its presence on that cloth. This much we know: there is no gaseous or liquid diffusion migrating into the fibers, no pigment particles deposited on the threads, and no visible brush strokes, which indicate the image was definitely not painted on the cloth."

Clearly, the evidence the scientists have uncovered thus far is, if anything, more exciting and challenging than ever. It is no wonder that the final results should be so eagerly awaited.

Will the mystery of the Shroud ever be solved?

We might just assume, for the sake of the argument, that the scientists will one day discover that the Turin Shroud is not the authentic burial cloth of Jesus. Would this solve the mystery of the Shroud?

"No," replies a young American scientist. "If anything, we would have an even greater mystery on our hands. The question would still be there: 'Whence this incredible portrait?' "

As far back as 1903, French academician Yves Delage, a self-styled agnostic who had delved into the problem of the Shroud, gave an even more direct and emphatic reply. Berated by a member of the French Academy for asserting that the image on the Shroud could be none other than Christ's, Delage replied: "Then, I dare you prove to me that it is not Christ's. But let me tell you, *mon ami*. You will have a far more difficult time to prove that the Man on the Shroud is not Christ than I had in order to prove that He is indeed Christ!"

The Church has invited and welcomed the scientists, and has literally placed her precious relic in their hands. Some timid soul objected: "What if? . . . " But a courageous Archbishop had the answer.

"Let the scientists in," he said. "Is the Church to be frightened by science? Or the truth? Whatever their verdict, our faith in Christ does not stand or fall with the Shroud!"

The Archbishop of Turin echoed the words of Pope Paul VI who, shortly before he died, reiterated what he had said years ago. "Let the scholars and scientists have full freedom for research . . . Whatever the judgment they will express about this surprising and mysterious relic, we cannot but wish that all who see it, looking beyond the exterior and mortal features of the Saviour's marvelous portrait, may be led to a clearer vision of His inmost and fascinating mystery."

For most people, the mystery of the Shroud will never be solved anymore than the mystery of Jesus Himself will be. A great many of them would prefer it that way. They say: "Let the Jesus of both the Gospels and the Shroud continue to challenge the minds and bestir the hearts of men.

For others, the mystery of the Turin relic

is no mystery at all. As they look at the face of the Man of the Shroud, they need not be told that it is a face no artist could have painted. They know instinctively that it is unlike anything iconography ever gave the world. To them it is a wonderfully familiar face, overpowering in the calm, serene majesty of death. They look at it and say quite simply: "It is the Lord!"

ABOUT THE AUTHOR

Father Peter Rinaldi, S.D.B. is one of the world's leading authorities on the Holy Shroud. As a seminarian he viewed the Shroud in his native city of Turin. As a priest he has labored tirelessly to promote interest in the Shroud and obtain the scientific community's participation in the discussion of its authenticity.

The recent exposition of the Holy Shroud at Turin, Italy, in 1978 and the subsequent series of sophisticated tests performed on the Shroud were a direct result of Father Rinaldi's visits to Humberto, King of Savoy, Pope Paul VI, and the Archbishop of Turin. He was responsible for bringing the Shroud to the attention of American space engineers from NASA and the Air-force Academy, and it was he who arranged for the presence of famous scientists from around the world at the 1978 exposition.

As pastor emeritus of Corpus Christi Church in Port Chester, New York, Father Rinaldi has constructed America's most beautiful shrine to Christ of the Holy Shroud and filled the hearts of thousands of pilgrims with his own deep love for Christ of the Passion.

A Salesian of Saint John Bosco, Father Rinaldi belongs to a religious family with a hundred year tradition of interest and promotion of the Church's most famous relic.